LENNOX
LEWIS

MARTYN TULLEY

LENNOX LEWIS

A PUGILISTIC HISTORY

pitch

First published by Pitch Publishing, 2017

Pitch Publishing
A2 Yeoman Gate
Yeoman Way
Worthing
Sussex
BN13 3QZ

www.pitchpublishing.co.uk
info@pitchpublishing.co.uk

A CIP catalogue record is available for this book from the British Library.

ISBN 978-1-78531-329-5

Typesetting and origination by Pitch Publishing

Printed in the UK by TJ International Ltd.

Contents

Abbreviations

BBBC	British Boxing Board of Control
DIS	Disqualified
EBU	European Boxing Union
HBO	Home Box Office
IBF	International Boxing Federation
IBO	International Boxing Organisation
J.BURG	Johannesburg
KO	Knockout
MC	Master Of Ceremonies
PTS	Points
RSC	Referee Stopped Contest
S.AFRICA	South Africa
TKO	Technical Knockout
US	United States
USA	United States Of America
USBA	United States Boxing Association
WBA	World Boxing Association
WBC	World Boxing Council
WBO	World Boxing Organisation
WBU	World Boxing Union

In memory of James, John,
Edward, Bill and Harry Tulley.
All of whom definitely knew a
left hook from a right cross.

Although in several of Lewis's world title contests there may also have been lesser-known versions of the championship at stake, only the main governing bodies have been listed in both the book text and his official career record.

Please note: In August 2014, Lewis's former manager Frank Maloney announced that he intended to undergo gender reassignment and would subsequently become known as Kellie Maloney. However, to avoid any unnecessary confusion, throughout this book the name of Frank Maloney will be used in reference to this person because that is the name she was known by at that time.

Introduction

WHEN an English-born 23-year-old wearing a Canadian vest won the super-heavyweight gold medal at the Seoul Olympics in October 1988, few could have imagined that he would go on to be ranked alongside the greatest heavyweights of all time. His name was Lennox Lewis.

No sooner had he beaten the highly rated American Riddick Bowe in the final at the Chamsil Students Gymnasium than Lewis was being courted by many of the world's top managers and promoters, particularly in the United States.

So it was a big surprise when Lewis decided to turn professional in the land of his birth and even more surprising that he did so under the guidance of Frank Maloney, then a relatively obscure figure in the world of big-time boxing.

On 27 June 1989, eight months after his Olympic triumph, Lewis beat a journeyman fighter named Al Malcolm in London to launch what was to become an eventful – and at times rocky – 14-year journey.

It was an odyssey that would see Lewis go on to win the British, Commonwealth and European titles, and take him all the way to the pinnacle of his sport as a three-time heavyweight champion of the world. Lewis ended his career universally regarded as the best heavyweight of his generation.

But like all journeys, it was not always smooth. Along the way, he encountered his share of battles, setbacks and controversies, both inside and outside of the ring. The aim of this book is not to deliver an unofficial biography of Lewis's life but concentrate on his fights in the ring, giving an in-depth history of the self-proclaimed 'Pugilist Specialist' that was Lennox Lewis.

The Early Days

BORN in Stratford, east London, England on 2 September 1965, Lennox Claudius Lewis was the second son of Violet Lewis. She had moved to London from her native Jamaica nine years earlier in search of a better life. Lennox and his older brother Dennis were born to two separate fathers and Violet decided to bring up her boys alone. As a single parent who also held down a nursing job at East Ham General Hospital, times were hard. Later, it was agreed that to ease Violet's burden Dennis would go and live with his father whilst Lennox remained with her.

Violet eventually travelled to America, where she spent a year in Chicago. Although many of her friends from Jamaica had settled there she did not qualify for a green card, which meant she was unable to work legally in the United States. As a result, she found it difficult to make any sort of life for herself. When she received news that Lennox, who had remained in London with his aunt Gee, had got into trouble fighting at school, she left Chicago and returned to London.

Later, Violet decided to leave England for a second time and try her luck in Kitchener, a manufacturing city in Ontario, Canada. On this occasion, though, she took the young Lennox with her.

Initially, things went well. Violet found a job in a factory, although her immigrant status meant she was forced to pay the full fees for Lennox's schooling. Combined with other factors, it became a struggle to get by.

It was decided that Lennox, who was still only seven and had only been in Canada for six months, should return to his aunt Gee in London until his mother got on her feet. He could then rejoin her in Kitchener, a place he loved.

Lennox's return took longer than expected. He spent five years in England, during which time he was forced to attend two separate boarding establishments for children considered unruly and troublesome. But Lennox also re-established his relationship with his brother and finally, at the age of 12, with his mother settled in Kitchener, he was reunited with her.

Upon his return to Canada, Lennox became friendly with a boy named Andrew Powis and with him began boxing at the Waterloo Police Boxing Association Gymnasium, run by a sergeant called Jerome McComb.

Eventually, Lennox was trained by a man named Arnie Boehm and under his guidance he became a skilful amateur boxer. Not only was Lennox naturally talented, he was also extremely dedicated. He never shirked training and was always willing to listen and learn.

He was later helped in his amateur career by a Romanian-born coach named Adrian Teodorescu, who was initially appointed as coach to the Canadian national boxing team before subsequently being promoted to head coach for the Canadian Seoul Olympic squad.

Lennox would eventually go on to enjoy a successful unpaid career, which saw him become the most celebrated fighter in the country's amateur boxing history.

In November 1983, the then 18-year-old Lennox travelled to San Domingo in the Dominican Republic to take gold at the World Junior Championships. The following year, Lennox also represented Canada in the super-heavyweight division at the Los Angeles Olympics, going out in the second round to eventual winner Tyrell Biggs (who he later beat as a professional).

Although Lennox was already being tempted by hefty financial offers to turn professional, he resisted the lure of money and instead set his sights on gold-medal glory at the Seoul Olympics in 1988.

After winning his first senior title at the Commonwealth Games in Edinburgh, Scotland in July 1986, Lennox's Olympic dream became a reality.

Having comfortably negotiated the early rounds in Seoul, Lennox was given a bye straight into the final when his semi-final opponent, a Pole named Janusz Zarenkiewicz, withdrew with a broken hand.

In the final, Lewis met the young American Riddick Bowe, who hailed from the same Brownsville district as Mike Tyson and prior to the Games had been declared a nailed-on favourite to win gold.

But Lewis cared little for reputations. In the second round, Lewis overwhelmed Bowe, forcing two counts and stopping the favourite on his feet. Lennox Lewis had arrived. Not only had he capped his already-impressive amateur career by becoming an Olympic champion, but the time was now right for him to capitalise on his success by turning professional.

Turning Professional

NOT surprisingly, winning the super-heavyweight gold medal at the Seoul Olympics had made Lewis a hot property. Originally, he was expected to turn professional with a group called Mallet Sports Inc., which was controlled by a Canadian businessman named David Hurst. Hurst was already involved with both Lewis and another Canadian boxer called Egerton Marcus, who had won middleweight silver in Seoul, thanks to a deal agreed several months before the Games.

But Lewis was advised to reject the deal with Mallet Sports Inc. and after considering several outstanding offers from a number of top managers and promoters worldwide, he eventually signed with an up-and-coming British outfit called World Sports Promotions.

The group was run by Ambrose Mendy and Frank Maloney, who were already handling the career of the exciting British middleweight

Nigel Benn. In order to back up what they were offering Lewis, Mendy and Maloney were forced to bring in another party with the necessary financial clout to make the deal work.

This role was filled by the Olympic Gold Group, a new sports arm of the already-successful Levitt Group, owned by a businessman called Roger Levitt. However, because of Mendy's criminal record and prison background, the Levitt Group was not overly keen to work with him.

Mendy then encouraged Maloney to try again with the Levitt Group on his own. Even though it had originally been Mendy who came up with the idea of approaching the Levitt Group for backing, on securing the deal of a lifetime Maloney felt he had no option but to leave Mendy behind.

The eventual deal struck was a fantastic one for all concerned. On 23 April 1989, Lewis, accompanied by his American lawyer John Hornewer, flew to London to sign the contracts.

The 6ft 5in Lewis was now all set to embark on his professional journey in Britain, which had not boasted a world heavyweight champion since Bob Fitzsimmons 90 years earlier.

Lewis was to be officially managed by Maloney, a 5ft 3in Cockney, and trained by John Davenport, a former US Marine drill sergeant who had a reputation for being a very hard taskmaster. Lewis was ready to go.

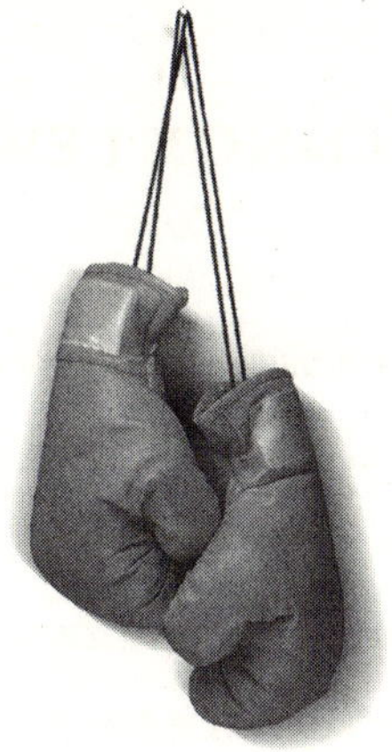

Fight 1

AL MALCOLM

Venue: Royal Albert Hall, London, England

Date: 27 June 1989

Scheduled rounds: Six

Weights: Lewis 231lbs; Malcolm 215lbs

Records: Lewis debut; Malcolm 11-12-1

Result: Lewis won KO2

LENNOX Lewis made his professional debut at the Royal Albert Hall in west London 268 days after winning the Olympic gold medal. He took on journeyman Al Malcolm on the undercard of a ten-round welterweight bout between the Scotsman Gary Jacobs and American Rollin Williams.

Malcolm, from Birmingham, was eight years older than Lewis at 31 and had lost half of his 24 contests, with one draw. Despite his poor record, he was the reigning Midlands Area champion, having won the vacant crown in January 1987 with a ninth-round stoppage of Ian Priest.

At 6ft 3in, Malcolm was only two inches shorter than Lewis but gave away over a stone in weight. Lewis looked in fantastic shape: long, lean and ready to do damage. Malcolm was an ideal first opponent: worthy but not too dangerous.

As expected, Lewis's paid bow didn't last long. Understandably keen to impress, Lewis dropped Malcolm with a left hook inside a minute and almost fell over himself trying to finish the fight as he pounded Malcolm all over the ring in the first round.

The fight ended unsatisfactorily just 19 seconds into round two when Malcolm tried to land a looping right hand and his forward momentum sent him face-first to the canvas. As he got up on to his knees, Malcolm began squinting and holding his glove up to his right eye, a position he was still in when the referee's count reached ten.

Lewis raised both arms aloft – a trademark pose that would become familiar throughout his career – and was declared the winner of his first professional fight.

Although Lewis had tried too hard to look good, there was plenty to be excited about. He had shown aggression, variety and punching power in the short time the fight lasted. Despite carrying his hands low, the power, talent and potential were undeniable. Lewis had taken his first step on a road that would eventually take him to the top of the world.

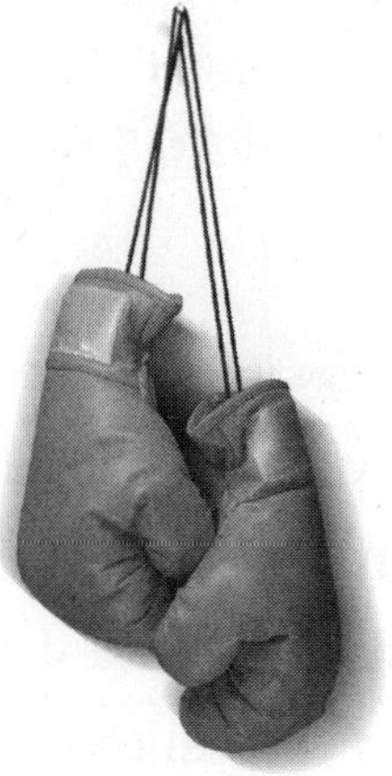

Fight 2

BRUCE JOHNSON

Venue: Convention Center, Atlantic City, USA

Date: 21 July 1989

Scheduled rounds: Six

Weights: Lewis 233lbs; Johnson 192lbs

Records: Lewis 1-0; Johnson 5-10-1

Result: Lewis won TKO2

BRUCE JOHNSON

IN his second outing in the paid ranks, Lewis was given an early opportunity to fight on a big world heavyweight title show in America. He was matched with the tall, lanky Bruce Johnson of Cleveland, Ohio, who looked about two weight divisions smaller than Lewis when they squared up in the ring. The bout took place on the undercard of Mike Tyson's ninth title defence against Carl 'The Truth' Williams, which lasted all of 93 seconds.

Johnson was a year younger than Lewis at 22 but had already been a professional for four years. Ominously, Johnson had lost ten of his 16 contests, including a first-round knockout by Oliver McCall, a tough, capable but unpredictable fighter Lewis would later run into himself. Johnson wasn't expected to be much of a test for Lewis and that's how it proved.

After the frenetic nature of his debut, Lewis looked to box more calmly behind his left jab, although Johnson was able to nullify him by keeping himself on the outside and crowding Lewis whenever he got into punching range.

In the second, Lewis switched his attack to the body, a tactic that paid dividends as he began to dominate Johnson. The American managed to bring a cheer from the crowd when he shot in a crafty right to Lewis's head when backed into a corner.

It was Johnson's only success as Lewis continued to rain punches on him, with a final overhand right sending the smaller man reeling and prompting referee Steve Smoger to stop the fight after 1min 24sec of the round.

Former world lightweight champion Jim Watt, doing ringside analysis for ITV, which screened the bout live as part of its overnight coverage of Tyson–Williams, said of Lewis: 'It was probably an improvement on his first performance but you can't really judge against a man like this.'

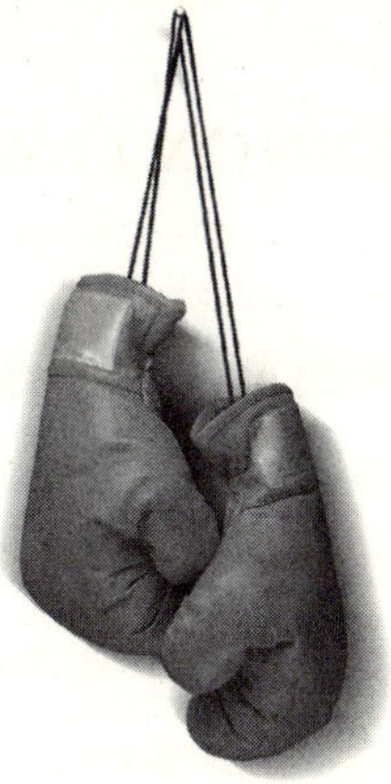

Fight 3

ANDY GERRARD

Venue: National Sports Centre, Crystal Palace, London, England

Date: 25 September 1989

Scheduled rounds: Six

Weights: Lewis 234lbs; Gerrard 225lbs

Records: Lewis 2-0; Gerrard 11-30-5

Result: Lewis won TKO4

AFTER his American bow, Lewis's handlers took him back to England for his third fight. His bout against the experienced Welshman Andy Gerrard was the headline attraction at the National Sports Centre, Crystal Palace, in south-east London, with TV coverage on the BBC. Gerrard was coming out of retirement to face Lewis, although he had only quit the ring three months earlier after a points defeat by Chris Jacobs for the Welsh heavyweight title.

But the chance of one last payday against Olympic champion Lewis was too good to refuse.

Gerrard came into the fight having won only 11 of his 47 contests but had proved himself a brave and durable opponent by extending former and reigning British champions Horace Notice and Gary Mason respectively. He had also twice lasted the distance with Glenn McCrory, who went on to win the IBF version of the world cruiserweight title.

Despite this, the 26-year-old wasn't expected to pose too many problems for Lewis. At 6ft 2½in, Gerrard had significant disadvantages in height and reach and was also giving away 9½lbs in weight.

As expected, it all proved too much for Gerrard as Lewis worked him over for three rounds before closing the show in the fourth. Lewis unloaded to back his opponent into a corner and a follow-up attack had the Welshman covering up. Referee Larry O'Connell had seen enough and jumped in to save Gerrard from further punishment.

Gerrard's most noteworthy contribution was his own version of the 'Ali shuffle' at the end of the second round, which drew laughter from the crowd. As Gerrard slipped back into retirement for good, little could he have known that Lewis would one day be mentioned in the same breath as The Greatest.

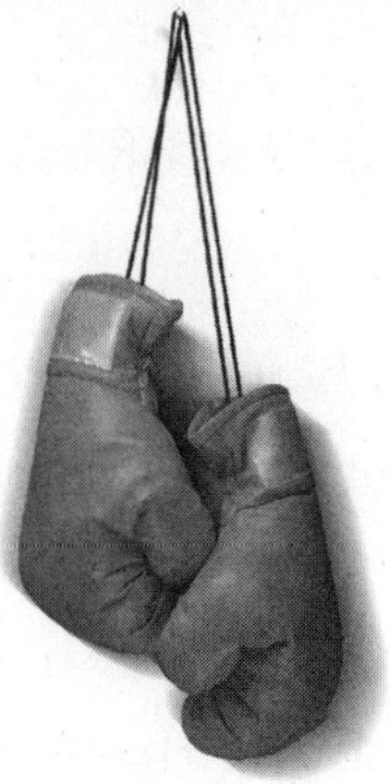

Fight 4

STEVE GARBER

Venue: City Hall, Hull, Yorkshire, England

Date: 10 October 1989

Scheduled rounds: Six

Weights: Lewis 232lbs; Garber 224lbs

Records: Lewis 3-0; Garber 13-10-1

Result: Lewis won TKO1

STEVE GARBER

AFTER his strong showing against Andy Gerrard, Lewis was back in action just 16 days later against Bradford's Steve Garber in Hull. At 6ft 6in, the 27-year-old Garber was marginally taller than Lewis and had a record of 13 wins from 24 fights. He came into the bout on the back of a stoppage victory over Joe Threlfall five months earlier and was on a winning roll, with four victories in his previous five outings.

During referee Ron Hackett's pre-fight instructions, Garber made the mistake of goading Lewis by rubbing his nose into his face. Lewis pushed Garber away in anger – and worse was to come. A right had Garber down inside a minute and although he managed to get up at four he was soon back on the floor from another right.

To his credit, Garber was still trying to rise again when the referee's count reached ten. It had taken Lewis just 90 seconds to secure his fourth straight victory. 'He beat me up,' Garber told Bob Mee of *The Telegraph* years later. 'He hit me so hard I could hear my ancestors in Africa.'

There were a few jeers mixed in with cheers, probably from those who felt they hadn't had their money's worth. But as easy as he was making things look, Lewis could only beat the man in front of him. Tougher tests lay ahead.

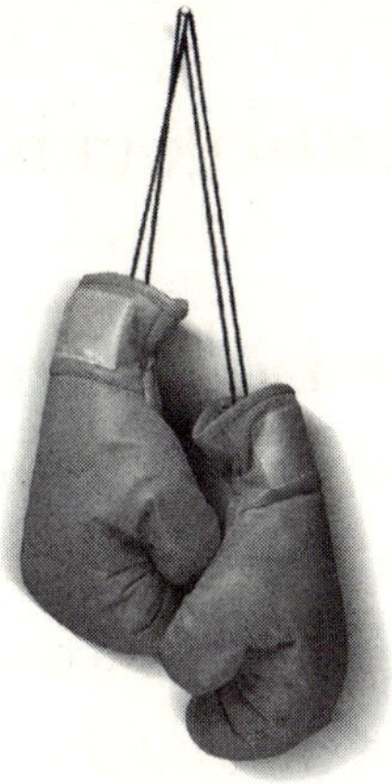

Fight 5

MELVIN EPPS

Venue: Royal Albert Hall, London, England

Date: 5 November 1989

Scheduled rounds: Six

Weights: Lewis 230¾lbs; Epps 193¾lbs

Records: Lewis 4-0; Epps 14-19-1

Result: Lewis won DQ2

WITH four inside-the-distance wins under his belt, and his potential becoming more evident with every fight, things were going well for Lewis. Although he had won Olympic gold for Canada, the London-born fighter was aiming to become the first British boxer to win the world heavyweight titles in nearly 100 years. But Lewis needed the support of the British public, the vast majority of whom had never heard of him before he turned professional. Lewis's next bout, against New Yorker Melvin Epps, did nothing to help.

The fight took place on the undercard of Azumah Nelson's WBC super-featherweight title defence against Londoner Jim McDonnell and was the first of Lewis's bouts to be shown on Screensport, a pan-European TV channel that later merged with its satellite rival Eurosport.

Although standing 6ft 3in, the 29-year-old Epps was giving away a massive 37lbs in weight but he was vastly more experienced than Lewis, having been a professional for ten years.

Epps had extended Renaldo Snipes and former light-heavyweight champion Eddie Mustafa Muhammad in his previous two fights, but had managed only 14 wins from his 34 contests overall. One of those was a six-round points victory over the former British and Commonwealth heavyweight champion Trevor Hughroy Currie in London three years earlier.

From the start, the fight was a messy, bad-tempered affair, with Lewis warned twice in the first round for low punching as he desperately tried to overpower his much smaller opponent. Epps did little but run, grab and hold and incurred the wrath of referee Tony Walker more than once. After another reprimand early in the second round, Epps was controversially disqualified, bringing the untidy maul to a halt.

With Epps outraged, the crowd voiced their disapproval by booing and showering the ring with paper cups. It had been the least satisfying victory of Lewis's career so far and also the least impressive. He had looked clumsy and impatient, showing little of the technique or natural talent of his Olympic days. In fact, Lewis had fought more like a novice than a potential contender for Mike Tyson's crown. Worse still, the public seemed to be against him – but there was still plenty of time to repair the damage.

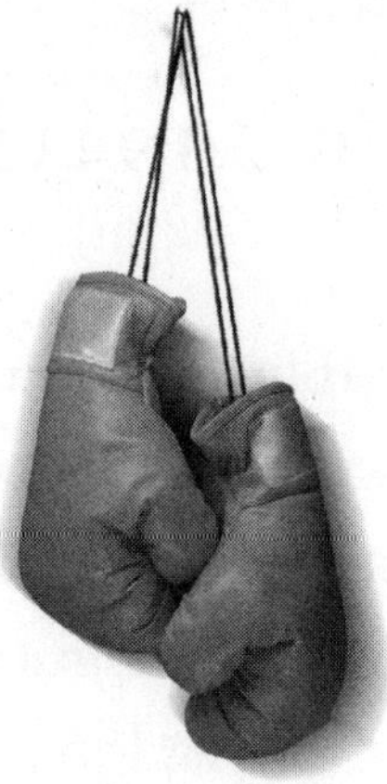

Fight 6

GREG GORRELL

Venue: Memorial Auditorium, Ontario, Canada

Date: 18 December 1989

Scheduled rounds: Eight

Weights: Lewis 226½lbs; Gorrell 206lbs

Records: Lewis 5-0; Gorrell 21-7

Result: Lewis won TKO5

GREG GORRELL

ALTHOUGH the aim was to build Lewis into a top heavyweight contender in Britain, he was taken back to Canada for his sixth fight. He received a rousing reception from the 4,500 crowd, especially when he was introduced as hailing from Kitchener.

Greg Gorrell, a 31-year-old from Kansas, had a decent enough record of 21 wins from 28 contests but had never met anyone of Lewis's calibre. At just 5ft 11in, Gorrell was considerably shorter than Lewis and, like the Olympic champion's previous professional opponents, was heavily outweighed.

The difference in size and physical condition was blatantly apparent, with Lewis looking athletic while the American was thick around the waist. The fight was one-sided. Lewis dumped Gorrell on the canvas at the end of the first round but, in contrast to the Melvyn Epps fight, seemed in no hurry to end it.

In the third, booing could be heard in some sections of the crowd as Lewis dropped the pace further. That encouraged the game Gorrell to try and make a fight of it, but he just didn't have the power to make a dent in Lewis.

The end came soon enough. Lewis, who had been chastised by trainer John Davenport at the end of the fourth round, came out for the fifth with his old menace back.

He unloaded a salvo of punches before several hard rights sent Gorrell down on to his knees. Although he was up at six, Gorrell was badly shaken and bleeding heavily from a cut over the left eye. It was enough for the referee to stop the fight in Lewis's favour after 51 seconds of the round.

Lewis's promoter Frank Maloney praised his man's performance, particularly his punch variety, although there must have been concern about how Lewis paced the fight. At times, he appeared to switch off.

The fight was remembered nearly 30 years later after Gorrell was tragically killed in a road accident in May 2016. 'His claim to fame is he fought Lennox Lewis,' Melissa Ramon, Gorrell's daughter, told the *Wichita Eagle*. 'Of course, he lost. That was always kind of a joke we made about it. But he fought him really hard.'

There would be much harder fights to come for Lewis, but they were still a way off yet.

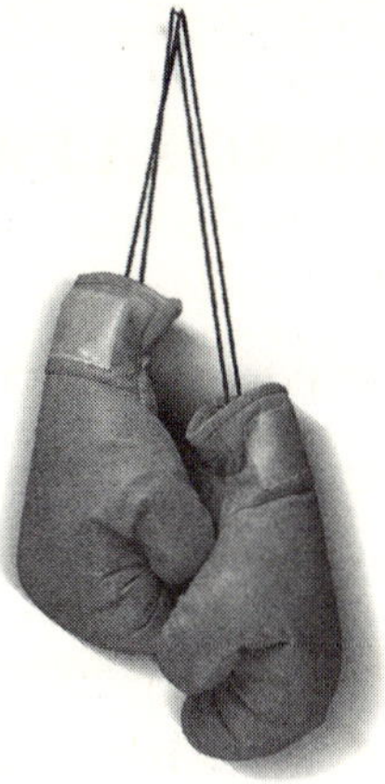

Fight 7

NOEL QUARLESS

Venue: York Hall, London, England

Date: 31 January 1990

Scheduled rounds: Six

Weights: Lewis 234lbs; Quarless 221lbs

Records: Lewis 6-0; Quarless 19-11

Result: Lewis won KO2

LEWIS'S first contest of the New Year was a definite step up in class. Liverpool's Noel Quarless was just three years older than Lewis at 27 but very experienced, having made his debut at 19 back in 1981. He had since amassed a record of 19 wins from 30 contests, with 11 inside the distance.

As his record suggested, Quarless was a hot-and-cold fighter but he had scored some decent wins over men like John L. Gardner, the Swede Anders Eklund and former WBA heavyweight champion John Tate. A victory over the much-touted Lewis would undoubtedly be the biggest of his career so far.

Quarless looked in decent shape physically and ready to go the full six rounds if required. Unfortunately, Lewis was in no mood to let him get that far.

Although Quarless made Lewis blink with a right hand in the first round, it proved to be a false dawn for the Liverpudlian. Lewis stayed calm and appeared to be visibly holding back as he waited for his chance.

It arrived in the second round. Lewis suddenly hurt Quarless and showed clinical finishing power to floor his opponent twice with his trademark right, the second time leaving him spreadeagled on the canvas. Quarless got up and argued angrily with the stoppage, but it was all over after one minute 20 seconds of the round. Lewis had win number seven.

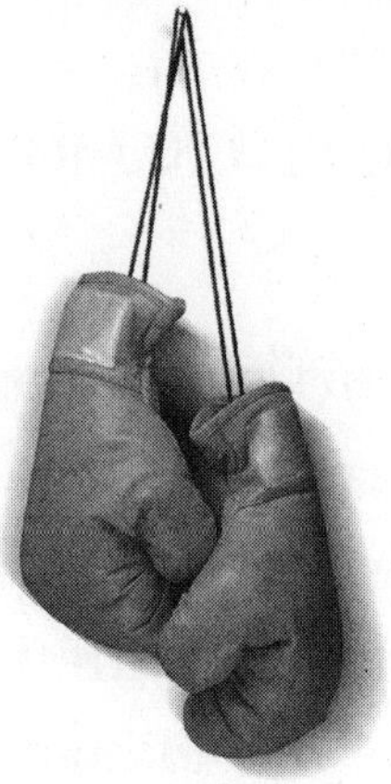

Fight 8

CALVIN JONES

Venue: Gateshead Leisure Centre, England

Date: 22 March 1990

Scheduled rounds: Eight

Weights: Lewis 233lbs; Jones 243lbs

Records: Lewis 7-0; Jones 13-4

Result: Lewis won KO1

FOLLOWING his impressive win over Quarless, Lewis had been set to meet the 6ft 6in Zimbabwean Proud Kilimanjaro in a top-of-the-bill clash at the National Sports Centre, Crystal Palace, London on 26 February 1990. The bout was planned as an official eliminator for the Commonwealth heavyweight title. With Kilimanjaro – real name Proud Chinembiri – at No 29 in the WBC ratings, he would have been the first world-ranked fighter Lewis had faced.

Alas, the fight fell through when Kilimanjaro refused to reveal the results of a pre-fight AIDS test, leaving the BBBC with no choice but to refuse him permission to box.

Lewis's manager Frank Maloney desperately tried to save the main event by bringing in Welshman Chris Jacobs as a late substitute, but bad weather made it impossible for him to get to the arena on time.

As a result, Lewis was pulled off the bill and was instead matched with the American Calvin Jones on 22 March 1990. The fight was chief support to the IBF cruiserweight title bout between Glenn McCrory and Jeff

Lampkin, which McCrory lost on a third-round stoppage. Jones himself was a six-day substitute for another American, Mike Cohen, and had only arrived in Britain the day before.

Jones, a former social worker, had 13 wins from 17 fights and had fought in good company. Three of his four losses had come against former world champions John Tate, James 'Bonecrusher' Smith and Tony Tucker.

The visitor, from Bristol, Tennessee, had fought and won just 12 days before facing Lewis, who was meeting an opponent bigger than himself for the first time since turning professional.

Lewis, though, wasted no time chopping Jones down to size, flooring him twice for a first-round stoppage.

Lewis's follow-up assault, which saw him club Jones to the floor, showed once again what a ruthless finisher the British prospect was becoming.

The brief bout was screened live on the Eurosport TV network and afterwards Lewis told viewers: 'I surprised myself with my own power because I hit him and all of a sudden he started wobbling. Then I thought: "Hey, I've got a punch behind me."

There could be no doubting Lewis's power but the other pieces of the jigsaw had still to be slotted into place. No one yet knew how Lewis might react when he was hit back or how his stamina would hold up in a longer fight in which the opponent was competitive. He would reach the top before either of those questions were answered.

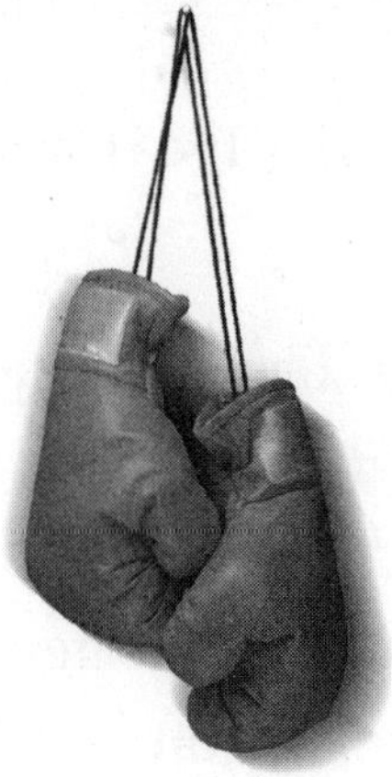

Fight 9

MIKE SIMUWELU

Venue: Royal Albert Hall, London, England

Date: 14 April 1990

Scheduled rounds: Eight

Weights: Lewis 233½lbs; Simuwelu 229lbs

Records: Lewis 8-0; Simuwelu 18-2-1

Result: Lewis won KO1

MIKE SIMUWELU

LEWIS'S ninth professional bout was another eight-rounder and for the second fight running he was the chief support to a world title contest, this time Londoner Michael Watson's unsuccessful challenge for Mike McCallum's WBA middleweight crown.

On paper, Zambian Mike Simuwelu had a respectable record of 18 wins from 21 fights, even though the quality of some of his opponents was questionable. Nevertheless, he was a former holder of the African heavyweight title having stopped Proud Kilimanjaro in August 1987 before losing to the same man 12 months later.

It was a potentially dangerous fight for Lewis as Simuwelu had scored all but one of his victories inside the distance, although he had been inactive for 11 months.

Lewis now needed some rounds after his string of quick wins to prepare him for tougher tests ahead, but it was a risky strategy against a puncher like Simuwelu.

In the event, it was business as usual for Lewis. He hurt Simuwelu with a right after about 30 seconds before a combination, ending with a stunning left hook, sent the African crashing down. Badly dazed, Simuwelu tried bravely to rise but was counted out after just 58 seconds of the first round.

Lewis was now on a roll. He had won seven of his nine professional fights inside two rounds and had spent less than 20 rounds in the ring in total. He had simply been too big and strong for all his opponents so far, but there was still no telling how he would fare when the going got tougher.

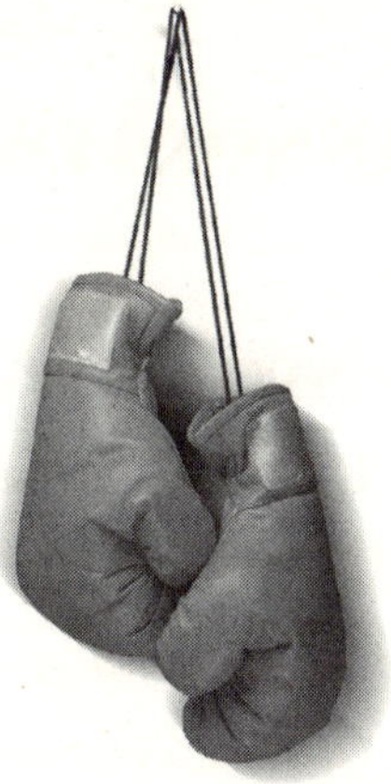

Fight 10

JORGE DASCOLA

Venue: Royal Albert Hall, London, England

Date: 9 May 1990

Scheduled rounds: Eight

Weights: Lewis 232½lbs; Dascola 223½lbs

Records: Lewis 9-0; Dascola 14-3

Result: Lewis won KO1

JUST 15 days after his quick win over Mike Simuwelu, Lewis was back at the Royal Albert Hall to face another substitute opponent in Argentinian Jorge Dascola in a live Wednesday night fight that was shown on ITV.

Dascola, who was brought in to replace American Lionel Washington, had been a professional for six and a half years and amassed a decent record of 14 wins from his 17 contests. The first 16 of those bouts had all taken place in his homeland and Dascola's only foray outside his own country ended in a creditable 11th-round stoppage loss at the hands of the former WBA heavyweight champion Michael Dokes.

Even though Lewis was topping the bill, the arena was less than half full with Kirkland Laing challenging the Frenchman Antoine Fernandez at the Wembley Conference Centre the same night.

Dascola appeared thick around the middle and those in attendance must have wondered just how well prepared he was to face Lewis.

Any reservations were justified when Lewis put Dascola down inside the first six seconds.

The visitor got up but already it looked only a matter of time before he was put out of his misery.

The finish, when it came, was untidy as Lewis clubbed Dascola with three right hands on the back of the head to send him down near the ropes, where he was counted out in the act of rising with just one second left in the round.

Not for the first time at a Lewis fight, the crowd booed. It was Lewis's third first-round win in a row and his fights were becoming repetitive. He seemed content to steamroller opponents rather than use his boxing skills. A bit more polish was needed.

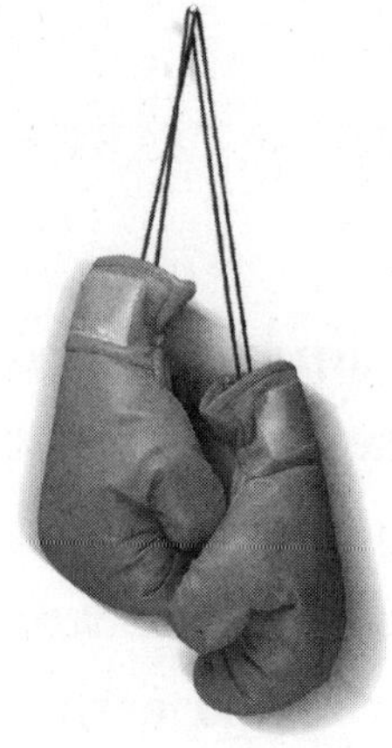

Fight 11

DAN MURPHY

Venue: City Hall, Sheffield, England

Date: 20 May 1990

Scheduled rounds: Eight

Weights: Lewis 230½lbs; Murphy 210¾lbs

Records: Lewis 10-0; Murphy 25-4-1

Result: Lewis won TKO6

DAN MURPHY

LENNOX Lewis was now unbeaten in ten fights but the jury was still out on him. The British public had seen him box a total of 21 rounds against opponents who hadn't put up much resistance. Even though in some fights he had shown glimpses of his undoubted talent and power, in others he had looked crude and impatient. With all his victories coming inside the distance, fans were still waiting to find out how Lewis would perform against someone more durable.

Just 11 days after the win over Jorge Dascola, Lewis was back in action against an American called Dan Murphy, yet another substitute opponent, who had come in for original choice Phil Brown.

Murphy, from Omaha, Nebraska, had served as a sparring partner for the former world heavyweight champion George Foreman and won all but five of his 30 contests. But one of his three defeats had been a first-round stoppage at the hands of Mike Simuwelu, who had been wiped out by Lewis the previous month. The formline didn't look good.

In reality, Murphy was little more than a blown-up cruiserweight. He knew there was no way he could match Lewis for strength and not surprisingly spent most of the six rounds he lasted running, holding or covering up.

By the sixth, referee Ron Hackett had seen enough with Murphy, bleeding from the nose and badly cut under the left eye, getting battered in a corner.

The fight did little for Lewis's reputation. The only redeeming aspect was that he had gone beyond five rounds for the first time. It was still no test, though, as Murphy had spent most of the fight just trying to survive.

The criticism over the standard of Lewis's opposition wasn't going away but the reality was it was no worse than that faced by past heavyweight champions such as Mike Tyson, Joe Frazier and George Foreman in the early part of their careers. Frank Maloney insisted Lewis was still learning and when he did eventually go for the world title, he would be ready to win it.

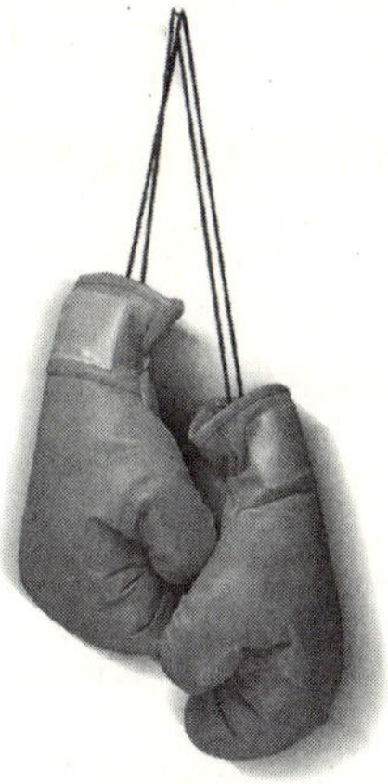

Fight 12

OSSIE OCASIO

Venue: Royal Albert Hall, London, England

Date: 27 June 1990

Scheduled rounds: Eight

Weights: Lewis 224lbs; Ocasio 229lbs

Records: Lewis 11-0; Ocasio 22-9-1

Result: Lewis won pts 8

LENNOX Lewis had now been a professional boxer for exactly a year but criticism over the quality of his opponents was growing louder. It was answered in his 12th fight when he was matched with the vastly experienced Puerto Rican Ossie 'Jaws' Ocasio.

The 34-year-old was a former WBA cruiserweight champion who had also challenged Larry Holmes for the WBC heavyweight crown in 1979. In 32 fights, Ocasio had lost nine times but only top men had beaten him. Apart from Holmes, who stopped him in the seventh round, it had taken fighters of the calibre of Evander Holyfield, Tyrell Biggs, Ray Mercer and Bruce Seldon to get the better of Ocasio, who had also managed a draw with ex-champ Michael Dokes.

Ocasio was easily the biggest name Lewis had met to date. A veteran in his 15th year as a professional, Ocasio was past his best but was just the sort of opponent Lewis needed at this stage in his career.

The visitor played his part to perfection. Although he never had Lewis in trouble, the crafty Ocasio knew enough to keep the fight competitive until the final bell. For the first time, Lewis showed respect to his opponent and was reluctant to take chances, preferring to box behind his jab for the most part. Ocasio seemed to shake Lewis with a right in the sixth but it wasn't enough to threaten an upset. Lewis responded and won 80-77 on the referee's scorecard – or three of the eight rounds with five even. It was the first time he had gone the distance.

Once again, booing could be heard from certain sections of the Albert Hall crowd. It was harsh on Lewis, who had just come through his hardest test against a tough, wily opponent and seemed to have plenty left at the end. Lewis had gone up several levels and although he hadn't shone he had still won handily. More importantly, he had probably learned more in this fight than in his previous 11 put together – and that had to be worth something.

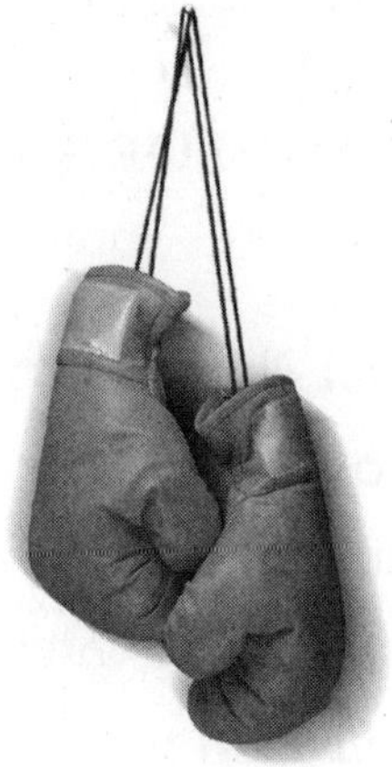

Fight 13

MIKE ACEY

Venue: Superstars Niteclub, Mississuaga, Ontario, Canada

Date: 11 July 1990

Scheduled rounds: Ten

Weights: Lewis 228lbs; Acey 221lbs

Records: Lewis 12-0; Acey 11-4-1

Result: Lewis won KO2

MIKE ACEY

THERE was never any danger of it being unlucky 13 for Lewis when he travelled back to Canada to face the hopelessly overmatched American Mike Acey in his first scheduled ten-rounder.

The reason Lewis, despite being based in Britain, was continuing to fight in the country where he had enjoyed such a successful amateur career was two-fold. It gave the Canadian public another chance to see the Olympic champion in action and also left the door open for Lewis to fight for the Canadian title, then held by Ken Lakusta.

The much smaller Acey tried to eyeball Lewis during the pre-fight instructions but he had virtually no chance of winning. Although all his wins had come by knockout, the most notable result on Acey's record was a first-round defeat at the hands of Lewis's old Olympic rival Riddick Bowe in October 1989.

The fight with Lewis was a dreadful spectacle. Acey came out aggressively but was put down four times before referee Harry Davis finally stopped the bout after 94 seconds of the second round.

'The crowd don't like this.... they came to see a fight and they're not going to get what they want here tonight,' local TV analyst Spyder Jones told viewers at the end of the first round.

In the second, Lewis flirted with disqualification after hitting Acey three times while he was down. It was another reminder that Lewis still lacked the maturity he would later develop, but on the whole he boxed a controlled fight against an opponent who was not in his class.

TV commentator Scott Grandville observed that Lewis's jab was similar to that of George Foreman, only quicker. Lewis also worked effectively to the body.

Aftewards, there was a clear hint that the days of pushover opponents were about to end when Lewis warned: 'There will never be another Mike Acey in the ring with me again. Never.'

Jones added: 'Give this kid [Lewis] time. He is going to develop into a world-class fighter. He was the best amateur in the world and there is no way that he can't develop into the best professional in the world.'

Lewis was now just months away from taking his first meaningful step on that path. His manager Frank Maloney immediately announced that Lewis would be challenging for his first title in his next fight – the European heavyweight championship held by the Frenchman Jean-Maurice Chanet.

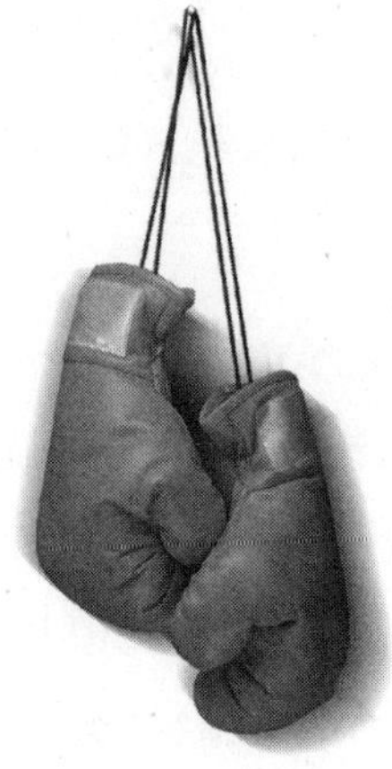

Fight 14

JEAN MAURICE CHANET

Venue: National Sports Centre, Crystal Palace, London, England

Date: 31 October 1990

Scheduled rounds: Twelve

Weights: Lewis 224lbs; Chanet 205¾lbs

Records: Lewis 13-0; Chanet 24-10

Result: Lewis won TKO6

LENNOX Lewis's first shot at a professional title had originally been planned for 7 October 1990, but was put back 24 days. By the time his fight with the Frenchman Jean-Maurice Chanet came around, Lewis had been out of the ring for three months – his longest inactive period since turning pro the previous year.

Chanet was the most unlikely looking of European champions. A balding, moustachioed gypsy fairground worker, he was really nothing more than a blown-up cruiserweight. His physique did not resemble that of a dedicated championship fighter. Indeed, he had once said his ambition in boxing was simply to earn enough money to give up his candyfloss stall on the Bois de Vincenner fairground and buy himself a more lucrative carousel.

Chanet was known in Britain, having twice beaten Londoner Derek Williams to win and retain the European title in France the same year.

The Frenchman had also fought Brits Dave Garside, Jess Harding and Andy Gerrard on his way to compiling a record of 24 wins in 34 fights. Lewis, though, was a different proposition entirely.

The bout, held on a Wednesday night, was nearly called off at the last minute when it was discovered a substance had been applied to the cut-prone skin above Chanet's eyes and liniment smeared on his body. BBBC secretary John Morris ordered the removal of both. He also insisted that Chanet's hands be rebandaged after it was found they had been taped up with his knuckles still showing.

At 36, Chanet was nine years older than Lewis and, like many of his opponents, was also giving away height and weight. As expected, the Frenchman wasn't in Lewis's league.

Cut on the bridge of the nose inside a minute, Chanet was already fighting an uphill battle. He gamely plugged away but couldn't get close enough to test Lewis, who dominated the first five rounds behind his jab and had Chanet in trouble every time he opened up.

By the end of the fifth, Chanet's face was a bloody mess and it was clear he wouldn't last much longer. A big right at the start of the sixth had Chanet covering up and another barrage of blows prompted the referee to step in and request a second inspection from the ringside doctor. With Chanet's injuries worsening, the fight was stopped after 21 seconds of the round.

At the age of 25, after just 14 professional fights, Lennox Lewis was the new heavyweight champion of Europe. Most agreed it had been the best performance of his career so far.

Having won his first major professional title, Lewis was now eyeing a double championship clash with unbeaten British champion Gary Mason – but not before first defending his European title against the Italian Cesare Di Benedetto at the Albert Hall on 5 December. In the event, Benedetto was withdrawn by the Italian Boxing Federation, meaning Lewis wouldn't fight again for over four months. It didn't matter. Lewis had now gone up a level and the big fights he craved were drawing closer.

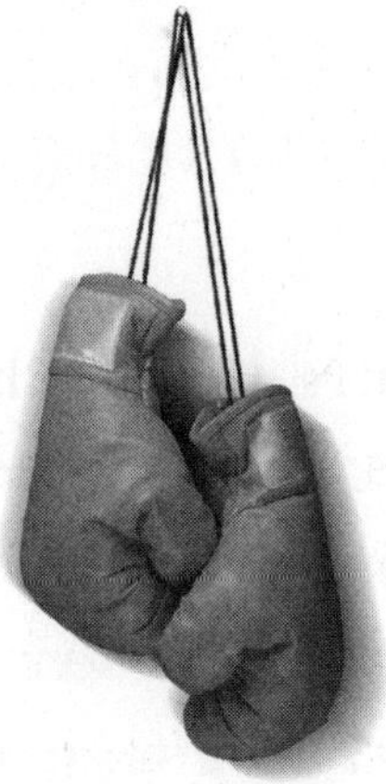

Fight 15

GARY MASON

Venue: Wembley Arena, London, England

Date: 6 March 1991

Scheduled rounds: Twelve

Weights: Lewis 227lbs; Mason 235lbs

Records: Lewis 14-0; Mason 35-0

Result: Lewis won TKO7

GARY MASON

WHEN Lennox Lewis and Gary Mason met in a battle of undefeated champions at Wembley Arena, it was billed as the biggest all-British heavyweight fight for 20 years. Not since the clash between Henry Cooper and a young, brash Joe Bugner at the same venue in March 1971 had two domestic big men squared off with so much on the line.

Two championships were at stake – Mason's British title and Lewis's European crown – and both knew defeat would cost them their place in the queue for a world title fight. But despite the risk involved, the fight made sense as Lewis and Mason were the leading contenders for each other's titles.

The promotional bidding war for the fight was won by Mason's manager Mickey Duff, who put up a record sum of £276,000, to be split equally between the two boxers.

Despite having had only 14 fights, Lewis was already ranked number 11 by the WBC, seven places below Mason. There was concern, though, that Lewis wasn't ready for the heavy-handed Londoner, who had scored 32 knockouts in 35 consecutive wins while largely fighting in the shadow of his better-known stablemate Frank Bruno.

Mason had suffered a detached retina in his right eye during a points win over Everett 'Big Foot' Martin a year earlier and was having only his second fight since undergoing corrective surgery.

Before the bout, which was screened live on BBC television, Mason showed no fear of Lewis's growing reputation by warning: 'Lennox keeps saying I've got something he wants. Well, I've got something I wanna give him.' Mason was presumably making a cryptic reference to his right hand, a formidable weapon with which he had knocked out many of his previous opponents. But it wasn't enough against Lewis.

Taller and more mobile, Lewis controlled the fight behind his long left jab as Mason battled to get inside, where he could do most damage. Mason was hampered from the third round onwards by a swelling around his right eye, which steadily worsened as he fought on bravely to try to turn the tide his way.

A last-ditch attack by a wounded and increasingly desperate Mason at the start of the seventh failed to save him. While separating the fighters from a clinch, referee Larry O'Connell decided to stop the fight with Mason's face a bloody pulp, his damaged eye completely closed.

At 25, Lewis was now the British and European heavyweight champion and it was still less than two years since he had turned professional. Although Mason had been the crowd favourite, Lewis's victory against a dangerous, unbeaten opponent had gone at least some way towards engendering the public approval he wanted as he moved towards bigger fights.

The significance of the fight with Mason was never forgotten by Lewis. In January 2011, nearly 20 years later, Mason was tragically killed in a road traffic accident while out riding his bicycle in south London. Remembering his rival, Lewis tweeted: 'My bout with him was a watershed moment in my career and I'm truly grateful to have known him.'

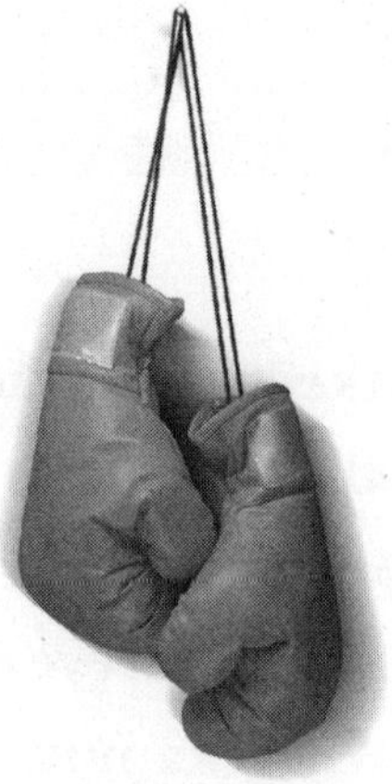

Fight 16

MIKE WEAVER

Venue: Caesars Tahoe, Stateline, Nevada, USA

Date: 12 July 1991

Scheduled rounds: Ten

Weights: Lewis 221lbs; Weaver 215lbs

Records: Lewis 15-0; Weaver 35-15-1

Result: Lewis won TKO6

THE stakes were gradually rising for Lennox Lewis. After a planned fight against James 'Bonecrusher' Smith fell through, Lewis was next matched with another former heavyweight champion in Mike Weaver outdoors at Caesars Tahoe, Nevada.

It was a fight that Lewis was expected to win, particularly as it represented his first major exposure in America. The scheduled ten-rounder was broadcast on TVKO, a pay-per-view platform owned by Time Warner, the parent company of cable network HBO. The aim now was to start building Lewis into a saleable contender for the world heavyweight title.

Despite being at the tail-end of his career, the 39-year-old Weaver was still a name and had kept himself in top condition. He had won the WBA heavyweight title 11 years earlier with a dramatic last-round knockout of John Tate and had also challenged Larry Holmes and Pinklon Thomas for the WBC title six years apart.

At his peak, Weaver had a reputation as a big puncher but he was also vulnerable himself. Holmes and Thomas had both stopped him and

Weaver had also been beaten in 63 seconds by Michael Dokes, although he recovered to fight his conqueror to a 15-round draw six months later.

Despite his age, Weaver was still considered a credible test for the developing Lewis, who needed to win convincingly with a five-fight US TV deal in the offing.

For five rounds, Lewis dominated behind a sharp jab, showing good movement and punch variety as the much slower Weaver soaked up everything the younger man threw at him. Then, in the sixth, Lewis found the punch he was looking for. Out of the blue, he unleashed a long, flashing right hand that sent Weaver crashing on to his back, where he was counted out. Even allowing for Weaver's advancing years, it was an impressive finish.

But Lewis still couldn't please everybody. In a column published a few months later, Pat Putnam of *Sports Illustrated* took a sarcastic swipe at what he perceived as Lewis's slow progress. 'Lewis has fought less than 58 full rounds and never more than eight in any outing,' wrote Putnam. 'Trying to toughen up with such light work is like trying to sharpen a knife with a bar of soap.'

It wouldn't be long before Lewis showed how tough he was – not that Weaver needed convincing. Recalling their fight in an interview with Joe Sebastinelli of *KO Digest* in January 2014, Weaver admitted: 'I hadn't fought in a while and I trained only a week or two for the fight. One possibility was that I could knock him out, but if somebody asked me about how I would do against Lennox, I would say "I'll do my best", but deep down inside, I knew I wasn't going to hang with him at that point in my life. I took the fight for money.'

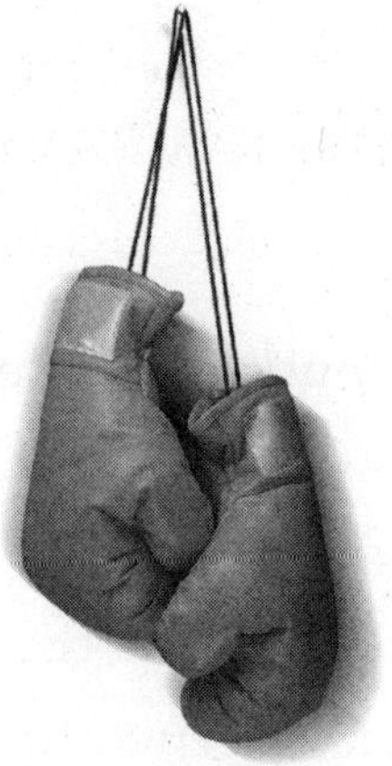

Fight 17

GLENN McCRORY

Venue: Royal Albert Hall, London, England

Date: 30 September 1991

Scheduled rounds: Twelve

Weights: Lewis 231lbs; McCrory 221lbs

Records: Lewis 16-0; McCrory 28-6

Result: Lewis won KO2

LENNOX Lewis's handlers had agreed a bout with Glenn McCrory, the former world cruiserweight champion, two months before the Weaver fight. It was originally expected to take place at the G-Mex Centre in Manchester but was shifted to the Royal Albert Hall, scene of many of Lewis's early victories.

The fight, a British and European title defence for Lewis, took place nine days after super-middleweight contender Michael Watson had suffered near-fatal injuries in his world title bout with Chris Eubank in London. Many in the boxing community expressed reservations about its timing, with the stricken Watson still fighting for his life in hospital.

The bout went ahead but it was a mismatch. McCrory, although tough and proud, was simply too small to mix it with Lewis. McCrory had campaigned unsuccessfully as a heavyweight in his early career before dropping back down to cruiserweight, where he outpointed the Kenyan Patrick Lumumba to win the IBF title in front of his home crowd at Stanley, County Durham in June 1989.

His reign lasted less than a year. Severely weakened by weight-making, McCrory was knocked out in the third round by the American Jeff Lampkin in his second defence and moved straight back up to heavyweight.

Despite previously sparring nearly 100 rounds with a peak Mike Tyson, McCrory was never in the fight with Lewis. In a horribly one-sided bout, Lewis battered McCrory from pillar to post in the first round before dropping the challenger twice and knocking him out in the second.

After the fight, Lewis told Gary Newbon of ITV Sport: 'I had a lot of confidence going into the fight and I wanted to be taken really seriously. I didn't think Glenn McCrory took me that seriously so I wanted to prove to him that this is what the heavyweight class is all about.'

In 2012, McCrory recalled his often chaotic preparation for fights, including the Lewis bout, in an interview with Mike Jones of *Livefight.com*. 'Lennox Lewis was the best heavyweight of the generation and there was me leaving a pub to fight him!' McCrory joked. 'I had a pub to run and was still the same; no gym, no trainer etc. It's hardly a winning formula, is it? I had a go [against Lewis] but obviously he was far too strong for me.'

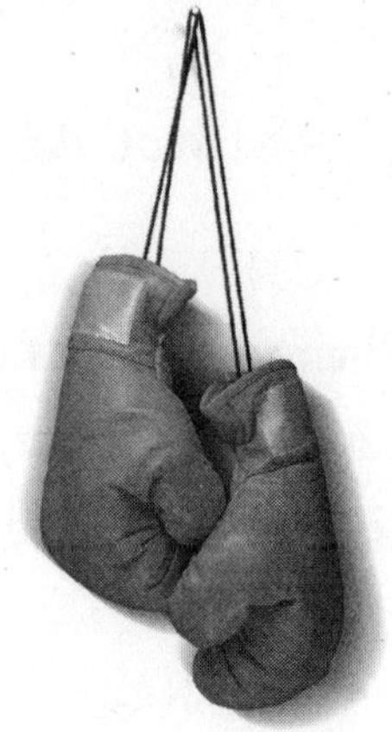

Fight 18

TYRELL BIGGS

Venue: Omni Arena, Atlanta, USA

Date: 23 November 1991

Scheduled rounds: Ten

Weights: Lewis 230½lbs; Biggs 231lbs

Records: Lewis 17-0; Biggs 19-4

Result: Lewis won TKO3

AFTER 17 straight wins, Lewis was now ranked highly by all four of the main boxing governing bodies. The WBA had him highest at number three, while the IBF, WBC and WBO all rated him in their top seven. In his next contest, Lewis was matched with the American Tyrell Biggs, who had beaten him on his way to the 1984 Olympic gold medal in Los Angeles.

The bout had originally been scheduled for the undercard of the Evander Holyfield–Mike Tyson world title clash in Las Vegas on 8 November 1991 before the fight was postponed when Tyson sustained a rib injury in training. It was later cancelled altogether after Tyson was charged with raping a contestant at a beauty pageant, where he was guesting as a judge. Tyson was subsequently found guilty and sentenced to six years in jail.

As a result, Holyfield got a new opponent, date and venue, a hometown defence against Francesco Damiani at the Omni Centre in Atlanta two weeks later. When the Italian pulled out with an ankle injury, Holyfield agreed to face a second substitute, Smokin'

Bert Cooper, with Lewis's fight against Biggs the chief support.

Lewis had unfinished business with Biggs. Seven years earlier, an 18-year-old Lewis had lost a unanimous decision to the American in the quarter-finals of the Los Angeles Olympics. Biggs went on to beat Damiani in the final and take the gold medal, and seemed destined for great things as a professional. He fell short, getting outclassed and stopped in seven rounds by Tyson in a premature title bid in Atlantic City in October 1987.

Although a standout amateur and a talented boxer, Biggs never appeared suited to the professional ranks. He was tall and fast but seemed to lack the natural strength and power to make it at the highest level. Biggs had further been troubled by a drug problem for which he had undergone therapy.

After the loss to Tyson, Biggs was never the same again. He became a trial-horse, a label reserved for faded fighters against whom young prospects measure their progress. Biggs was subsequently stopped by Damiani, who gained revenge for his Olympic defeat, British champion Gary Mason and Lewis's old amateur rival Riddick Bowe. In the fight with Bowe, Biggs had put up a decent showing, so Lewis was not taking him lightly.

The bout was shown live on HBO's *World Championship Boxing* program in America, giving Lewis the perfect platformme to advertise his championship credentials. He didn't waste it. Biggs looked intimidated from the start as Lewis came out aggressively, clearly intent on making a statement. In the third, he did it, flooring Biggs three times with right-handers to force an automatic stoppage under the three-knockdown rule.

HBO's Larry Merchant called Lewis a 'destroyer', and it was an accurate description. Lewis had got rid of Biggs five rounds faster than Bowe had managed and in the process delighted the small legion of fans who had travelled across the Atlantic from Britain to support him.

'The mission is to be world heavyweight champion,' an impassive Lewis told Merchant. 'All I need is a couple more fights and I'll be in there with the champion.'

It was a perfectly plausible scenario – but Lewis's emergence as a major force in the next 12 months would not happen in the manner he might have imagined.

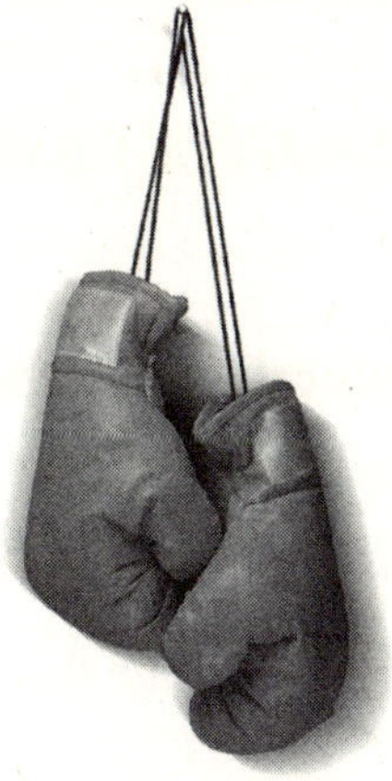

Fight 19

LEVI BILLUPS

Venue: Caesars Palace Sports Pavilion, Las Vegas, USA

Date: 1 February 1992

Scheduled rounds: Ten

Weights: Lewis 225lbs; Billups 228lbs

Records: Lewis 18-0; Billups 16-5

Result: Lewis won pts 10

AFTER his destruction of Tyrell Biggs, Lennox Lewis knew he needed to keep his profile in America high. He agreed to appear on a show in Las Vegas dubbed 'The Night of the Young Heavyweights', which would also feature fellow prospects Riddick Bowe and Michael Moorer. The omens didn't look good when Bowe pulled out after picking up an eye injury in training and things got worse when the Lewis camp couldn't find an opponent.

According to Lewis's manager Frank Maloney, former world champion James 'Bonecrusher' Smith and the dangerous but erratic Oliver McCall were among 15 different fighters approached to face Lewis. There was even talk of Lewis and Moorer facing each other before it was agreed that neither of them would benefit from such a fight at this stage of their careers.

Instead, in the nick of time, the job went to former American football player Levi Billups, of San Diego, while Moorer, who had given up his WBO light-heavyweight title to campaign as a heavyweight, was matched with Mike 'The Giant' White.

Billups, a former linebacker, had amassed 16 wins in 21 fights since turning to professional boxing at the late age of 26, having had no amateur experience. He was wide, squat and considerably shorter than Lewis, who knew that Billups had already been stopped inside three rounds by Moorer two years earlier. The incentive was to do the job more quickly.

It never looked likely. Lewis controlled the fight behind his jab but seemed content to pace himself through the ten rounds rather than go for a knockout. Billups soaked up Lewis's best punches, including a big attack in the last round, and fought back well in spurts. Lewis, though, had done enough to win comfortably on the judges' cards by scores of 100-90, 98-91 and 95-92.

Lewis had been nowhere near as impressive as he was against Biggs, but there were pluses. He had completed ten rounds for the first time and learned that not every opponent was going to buckle under his assaults.

After the Billups fight, the Lewis camp announced they were parting company with trainer John Davenport, whose unashamedly outspoken views on the British had done little to boost Lewis's popularity in his homeland. Lewis said the split had been amicable and tried to defuse the situation by claiming: 'I needed another outlook. It's like having a maths teacher and now it's time to learn English.'

Nevertheless, Davenport's noticeable lack of diplomacy could not have helped his relationship with Lewis. Davenport had said he regarded the British as inept when it came to boxing and had even gone as far as to say that God had 'taken all the dumb people in the world and dumped them in Britain'.

On top of this, the former marine's regimental style of doing things was also alleged to have annoyed Lewis, who was not overly keen on taking orders like an army recruit, especially when he was paying the wages.

Davenport was replaced by Puerto Rican Jose 'Pepe' Correa, whose main claim to fame had been his involvement with Sugar Ray Leonard, although it had not been continuous. Correa had worked with Leonard when the fighter was 14 but not resumed the association until the multi-weight world champion was 34 and well past his best. Nevertheless, Correa knew how to sell himself and got the Lewis job. The distinctive Correa, with his black-rimmed spectacles and droopy moustache, would be a prominent figure in Lewis's corner for the forseeable future.

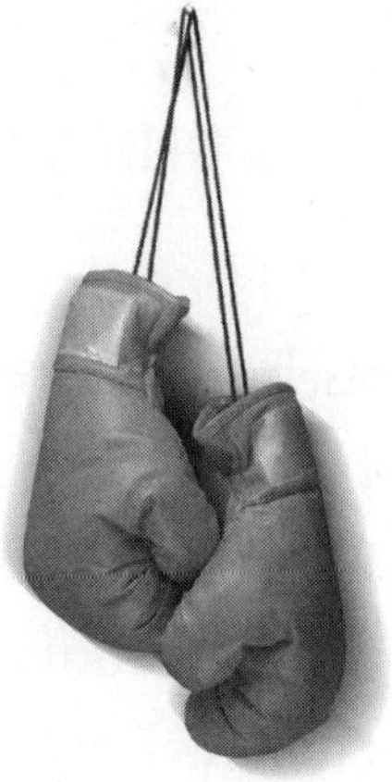

Fight 20

DEREK WILLIAMS

Venue: Royal Albert Hall, London, England

Date: 30 April 1992

Scheduled rounds: Twelve

Weights: Lewis 230½lbs; Williams 233lbs

Records: Lewis 19-0; Williams 19-4

Result: Lewis won KO3

IN his first outing under new trainer Jose Correa, Lennox Lewis put his British and European titles on the line in a triple championship clash with fellow-Londoner Derek Williams, who was defending his Commonwealth crown. It was the first time all three belts had been at stake in the same fight since Joe Bugner and Richard Dunne met in London on 12 October 1976.

Londoner Williams was a capable boxer who could also punch, and was Lewis's match physically at 6ft 5in. But Williams was also inconsistent. He had won and defended the Commonweath title impressively but lost two forgettable European title fights to Jean-Maurice Chanet – already beaten by Lewis – in France two years earlier.

In the first fight with Chanet, Williams's camp complained of illegal practices after their man, who had started promisingly, suddenly slipped into a trance-like state and lost a wide points decision. The European Boxing Union ordered a rematch but Williams performed terribly in the second fight and was outpointed again.

The big plus point for Williams coming into the fight with Lewis was the fact he had prepared in Florida under the tutelage of legendary trainer Angelo Dundee.

'Having worked with him, I realised he was definitely the right guy for the job,' Williams told Sky Sports shortly after Dundee's death in February 2012. 'It was a big fight, a big night, a big occasion and a big man in the corner. It was inspiring to know the kind of guys that Angelo had worked with like Muhammad Ali – the greatest of all time – and Sugar Ray Leonard and others. To be in that roll call of fighters was an amazing experience and feeling.'

For two rounds, Dundee's influence clearly helped Williams. He foiled, frustrated and at times outboxed Lewis, who neglected his boxing skills and simply tried to overpower Williams. In the second, Williams started grinning at Lewis and even patted him on the head with his right glove, a playful gesture that was immediately reciprocated.

The fun couldn't last, though. In the third, Lewis's strength was starting to tell and midway through the round he hurt Williams with a big overhand right. A pinpoint right uppercut then twisted Williams's head on his shoulders and

Lewis followed up instantly, landing two more punches to send his opponent down. Williams, wearing a look of resignation, was counted out in the act of rising.

Lewis had become the first man to stop Williams in 24 fights and was now a triple heavyweight champion. With the three belts strapped around his body, Lewis took the ring microphone to issue a challenge to the British public's favourite son Frank Bruno, who had just returned after a break of nearly three years following his world title defeat by Mike Tyson in Las Vegas.

In the post-fight interview with Sky's Paul Dempsey, there was more than a hint of self-satisfaction in Lewis's voice when he said: 'I wanted to show a lot of what Pepe showed me in the gym, but he said just go walk through him [Williams] and knock him out because he doesn't deserve to be in the ring with me.'

A blockbuster fight with Bruno was a natural but it was still a way off yet. Lewis had plenty of business to take care of first, including creating a seismic shock that no one saw coming.

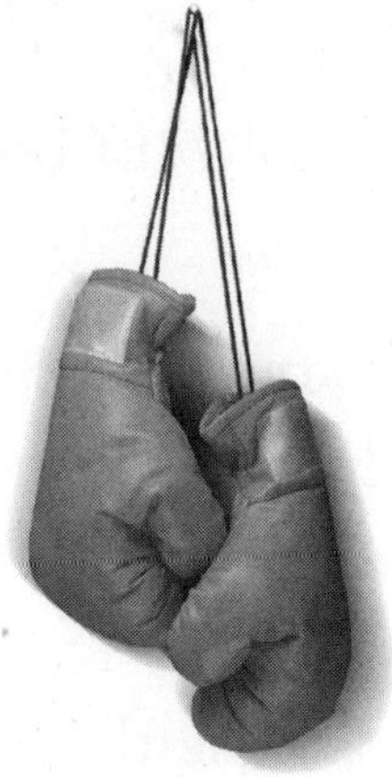

Fight 21

MIKE DIXON

Venue: Harrah's Casino, Atlantic City, USA

Date: 11 August 1992

Scheduled rounds: Ten

Weights: Lewis 233lbs; Dixon 207lbs

Records: Lewis 20-0; Dixon 10-5

Result: Lewis won TKO4

MIKE DIXON

THE month after his victory over Derek Williams, it was announced that Lewis would meet the dangerous Canadian Donovan 'Razor' Ruddock in an official eliminator for the WBC heavyweight title. The fight had arisen after the third-ranked contender Riddick Bowe rejected the bout, though the date and venue had still to be decided.

The original plan was for Lewis to keep busy by fighting on the undercard of the Rafael Pineda–Pernell Whitaker junior welterweight bout in Las Vegas on 18 July 1992. After further negotiations, it was decided that Lewis would face Ruddock at Earls Court, London on 31 October, but first box a warm-up in San Diego, California on 11 August. The bout was subsequently moved to Atlantic City, where Lewis was matched with the American Mike Dixon.

Dixon, of Atlanta, Georgia, was a small heavyweight but had mustered enough power to win ten of his first 11 fights inside the distance, half of them in the first round. The quality of his opponents, though, did not stand up to close scrutiny. By the time he met Lewis, Dixon had lost four in a row and wasn't expected to pose too many problems for the British contender.

The bout was being shown on *USA Tuesday Night Fights*, which meant for the first time Lewis would be seen live across America. At ringside, resplendent in a white suit, was Razor Ruddock, in attendance to weigh up the strengths and weaknesses of his next opponent.

During the build-up, Ruddock gave Lewis respect, telling TV anchorman Al Albert: 'I have to rank him up there with the rest of the heavyweights. He can punch, he won the Olympics. He warrants some respect. I will not take anything from him but I'm going to London to win.'

Ruddock could not have gleaned much from what he saw. Lewis had things all his own way in the four rounds the fight lasted, snapping out his jab and hitting his opponent almost at will with both hands.

At the start of the fourth, a thumping right knocked Dixon sideways and Lewis immediately followed up, forcing his man on to the ropes, where he proceeded to unload. Referee Rudy Battle stepped in to give Dixon a standing count but three more right hands from Lewis, the last of which buckled Dixon's knees, brought the one-sided bout to an end.

As expected, the American had not been much of a test or revealed anything about Lewis that wasn't already known. Afterwards, Ruddock told analyst Sean O'Grady: 'I can't take anything away from Lennox Lewis. I think he's graduated now to fight the number one contender and I'm going to oblige him on that. I'm going to let him see where he's at right now.'

Lewis said: 'I was just really taking my time and practising a couple of things. I was in no rush. I've got a recipe for Razor and on October 31 you're going to see Lennox Lewis take the edge off the Razor.'

Asked whether a fight with Ruddock had come too soon, Lewis said: 'I don't think so. There are a lot of unanswered questioned about Lennox Lewis and in the Razor Ruddock fight they can be answered.'

For a fighter who had still to face anyone in the top ten, those were brave words. But no one could have predicted the manner in which he would back them up.

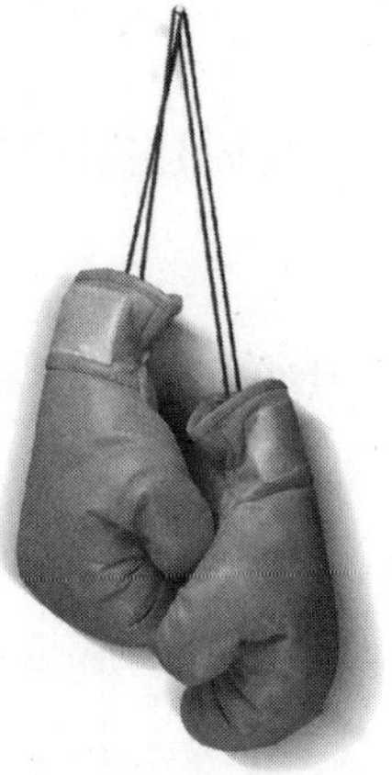

Fight 22

DONOVAN 'RAZOR' RUDDOCK

WBC heavyweight title final eliminator

Venue: Earls Court, London

Date: 31 October 1992

Scheduled rounds: Twelve

Records: Lewis 21-0; Ruddock 27-3-1

Weights: Lewis 227lbs; Ruddock 231½lbs

Result: Lewis won TKO2

LENNOX Lewis was now in deep. In agreeing to face Donovan 'Razor' Ruddock, he had reached the point of no return. Win and he would go on to fight for the world heavyweight title, at least theoretically. Lose and he would face the same sneering putdowns heard by every other British heavyweight of the previous 100 years. There was huge pressure on Lewis's broad shoulders, but he seemed oddly calm, as if he already knew exactly what was going to happen.

The fight, taking place in front of a capacity crowd on Halloween night, was a final eliminator for the WBC title, one of three held by the American Evander Holyfield. It also doubled as a first defence of Lewis's Commonwealth title, although that was almost irrelevant. What mattered was whether Lewis could deliver on the potential he had shown since winning the Olympic title four years earlier and become a legitimate challenger for the world heavyweight championship.

To clear the path to the Ruddock fight, Lewis had given up the European title, which he had been ordered to defend against Henry

Akinwande by 31 October. It was a small price to pay. Victory over Ruddock in front of a live TV viewing audience on both sides of the Atlantic (Sky Sports covered in Britain, HBO in America) would propel Lewis into the big league, where prestige and millions in purse money awaited.

'It's going to be a hell of a fight,' American boxing historian Hank Kaplan told Jonathan Rendall of *The Independent* the week before the fight. 'Ruddock is the heir apparent. In America you'll find the consensus is that Ruddock is the best heavyweight out of jail. Lewis is the brightest prospect around, the best defensive heavyweight in the world. It's a gamble. It's about who's betting the most.'

In Ruddock, Lewis was meeting not only the most dangerous opponent of his career but a man from a similar background. With his Jamaican roots and Canadian upbringing, Ruddock's early life mirrored his opponent's. As teenage amateurs, they had fought once, with Ruddock winning, and the pair had also sparred during Lewis's preparations for the 1984 Olympics.

As a professional, Ruddock had first come to notice with a devastating fourth-round knockout of former WBA champion Michael Dokes in New York in April 1990. But it was the following year that Ruddock really made his name.

In the space of three months, he fought on even terms in two brutal battles with Mike Tyson, surviving four knockdowns in total and a broken jaw in the rematch. Although he lost both fights, Ruddock emerged with his reputation enhanced.

By the time the Lewis fight came around, Ruddock's stock had risen further. With Tyson in jail after his rape conviction, Ruddock was regarded by many as the most dangerous heavyweight in the world and a perilous threat to Lewis.

Not everyone was convinced. As Ruddock entered the ring, HBO analyst Larry Merchant made the point that Ruddock's credibility had been based solely on two defeats. It was a salient one. Furthermore, Tyson, for all his ferocity, had clearly regressed in the two fights with Ruddock and still won them both. In Lewis,

Ruddock was now facing a fighter on the rise who had something to prove.

The general consensus among analysts was that in order to win Lewis would have to box with extreme caution, staying on the outside, well away from Ruddock's much-vaunted left hook. For most of the first round, Lewis did just that. Then, suddenly, he turned the tables. With about 20 seconds left in the round, Lewis landed a long, chopping, right hand that travelled in a downward arc, poleaxing Ruddock as if a rug had been pulled from under his feet. In an instant, the fight had changed. Ruddock got up, shocked and unsteady, and only the bell saved him from defeat.

Lewis needed no further encouragement. He came out aggressively in the second and immediately put Ruddock on the defensive. In no time at all, Ruddock was back on the floor, cowering under a hail of punches near the ropes.

The end was near and with cold, ruthless precision Lewis completed the execution with a frightening torrent of blows that left Ruddock sprawled face-first on the canvas for the third time. He looked up but the fight was over. Lewis had arrived.

Immediately after his crushing victory, a jubilant Lewis challenged Holyfield, who was two weeks away from defending his titles against the Briton's old Olympic rival Riddick Bowe. 'I am not just knocking on his door,' Lewis said. 'I kicked it down tonight.'

The overwhelming reaction of the British public, with whom Lewis had endured a mixed relationship, was not lost on the American media. Two days later, Ian Thomsen reported in the *New York Times:* 'Suddenly, Lewis, born in the London suburbs but raised a Canadian, was being swept high by a public famished for someone just like him, but until this moment skeptical that he was theirs.'

Accepted or not, Lewis was his own man and now a serious factor in the future of the heavyweight division. His accession to the throne, however, would not happen quite as he had planned.

WBC Champion

THE WBC eliminator between Lennox Lewis and Donovan 'Razor' Ruddock had been part of a four-way agreement in which Riddick Bowe would be permitted to challenge Evander Holyfield for his undisputed world heavyweight title. The understanding was that the winner would then defend against the winner of Lewis–Ruddock. When, just 13 days after Lewis's crushing victory over Razor Ruddock, Bowe relieved Holyfield of his belts via a 12-round points decision in Las Vegas, it was generally accepted that Bowe would make his first defence against Lewis.

In order to reinforce this, and to show they intended to honour the prior agreement, the WBC stated that the new champion and the Lewis camp should reach agreement by 13 December, or a further 15 days would be allowed while the bout went out to purse bids. Failure to comply would result in Bowe being stripped of the WBC title and Lewis being declared champion.

However, even before the bout, Bowe's manager Rock Newman had given signals that they might not go through with the original agreement. The month after his victory over Holyfield, with both Bowe and Newman in London, the manager accused the WBC of being corrupt. Before they could respond by stripping Bowe of their title, the American got in first by organising a press conference during which Bowe relinquished the WBC crown by throwing a replica of their belt into a rubbish bin. Bowe said that if Lennox Lewis wanted it, then he was nothing more than a 'garbage collector'.

Whatever the reasons behind Bowe's relinquishment of the title, the WBC were quick to react. On 14 December 1992, they announced Lewis as their new champion. The decision meant Britain, at long last, had a world heavyweight champion to call their own.

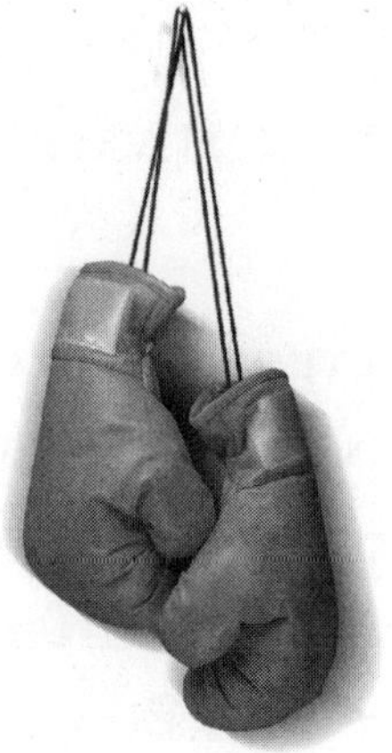

Fight 23

TONY TUCKER

WBC heavyweight title

Venue: Thomas & Mack Centre, Las Vegas, USA

Date: 8 May 1993

Scheduled rounds: Twelve

Weights: Lewis 235lbs; Tucker 235lbs

Records: Lewis 22-0; Tucker 48-1

Result: Lewis won pts 12

WITH the dust having settled on the stunning triumph over Razor Ruddock, and the victor's proclamation as the new WBC heavyweight champion, it was initially expected that Lewis would make his first defence against English-born Alex Stewart in March 1993, probably in Las Vegas.

However, at a boxing dinner on 14 January at the Marriott Hotel in London, where WBC president Jose Sulaiman officially presented Lewis with his championship belt, it was announced that the new champion would have to accommodate the organisation's number one contender, American Tony Tucker, next.

Six years earlier, Tucker had held the distinction of being the shortest-reigning heavyweight champion in history. Just 64 days after stopping James 'Buster' Douglas to win the vacant IBF title, Tucker lost it to Mike Tyson in the final of a year-long elimination series promoter Don King and cable TV network HBO had been running to find an undisputed champion.

Tucker, an intelligent boxer with a strong punch, had got into the series almost by default.

Michael Spinks, the reigning IBF champion, had been ordered to defend against Tucker but refused, preferring to take a more lucrative fight with white hope Gerry Cooney, for which he would earn a minimum of $4m. Spinks was stripped of his title and Tucker was matched with Douglas, a largely nondescript fighter who would shock the world less than three years later.

The fight with Douglas was a forgettable affair but Tucker made up for it against Tyson, fighting with admirable vigour despite going into the bout with a broken right hand. Tucker rocked Tyson with a left uppercut in the opening seconds and hung tough against the rampaging aggressor before losing a unanimous 12-round points decision.

Tucker was then out of the ring for more than two years, suffering drug-related problems and contractual disputes. He became a born-again Christian and returned to boxing under the guidance of Shelly Finkel, having been trained previously by the legendary Emanuel Steward, who would later greatly influence Lewis's career. Tucker subsequently won

14 fights in a row to claim the mandatory challenger's position, qualifying him for an automatic shot at Lewis. Tucker's promoter Don King won the purse bids, insisting on a 75-25 split instead of the usual 80-20 in favour of the champion. Despite this, Lewis was still guaranteed $9m to Tucker's $3m and must have felt some measure of reassurance when British officials Harry Gibbs and Mickey Vann were named among the three judges.

During the build-up, rumours surfaced that Lewis had badly injured his right hand in sparring, a murmur he initially denied but later confirmed was true. At 34, Tucker, of Grand Rapids, Michigan, was seven years older than Lewis but had far more experience and boasted almost identical physical dimensions. His record of 48 wins from 50 fights demanded respect but the Las Vegas oddsmakers weren't swayed and still had Lewis as a 6-1 on favourite the day before the fight.

'I think Lennox is a certainty to knock out or stop Tucker by the fourth or fifth round,' his manager Frank Maloney predicted at the final press conference.

It didn't happen. Lewis knocked Tucker down twice in the third and ninth rounds but couldn't finish him, frequently flailing wildly instead of picking his punches, as he had done against Ruddock. The bout became an untidy, laborious spectacle that raised questions about the legitimacy of Lewis's championship credentials. Lewis was forced to show heart in the eighth, fighting back to stagger Tucker after being hurt himself, but tired badly in the last quarter of the fight, when both boxers looked almost out on their feet. But Lewis had done enough. After 12 rounds, the furthest he had ever gone in a fight, Lewis was awarded a unanimous points decision, the judges posting scores of 118-111, 116-111 and 116-112.

On the whole, though, Lewis had not impressed. Ken Jones, ringside for *The Independent*, was scathing in his post-fight assessment. 'However you analyse cause and effect, this turned out to be a mediocre heavyweight championship contest, one that raised questions about Lewis's technique and stamina,' Jones wrote. 'If it is now established that he can withstand hard blows to the head and has the will to fight back strongly, too much of his work still bears the mark of an amateur. Lewis seemed incapable of putting more than two punches together and frequently failed to follow up an advantage.'

Next up for the unbeaten champion was the fight all of Britain wanted: a title defence against Frank Bruno. As expected, it was greeted with considerably less relish across the pond, where Pat Putnam of *Sports Illustrated,* in his latest Lewis critique, uncharitably described Bruno as a 'pantomimist with no particular fighting skills and a porcelain chin'.

Neither claim was true – Bruno was far better than generally given credit for – but despite Lewis's indifferent showing against Tucker the Londoner would still start a clear underdog in the Battle of Britain.

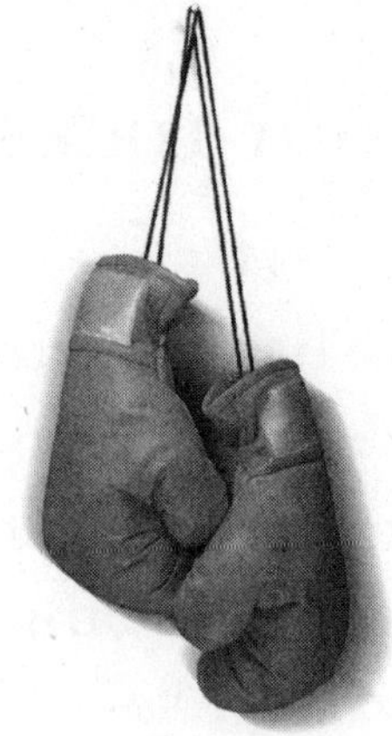

Fight 24

FRANK BRUNO

WBC heavyweight title

Venue: Cardiff Arms Park, Wales

Date: 1 October 1993

Scheduled rounds: Twelve

Weights: Lewis 229lbs; Bruno 238lbs

Records: Lewis 23-0; Bruno 36-3

Result: Lewis won TKO7

DESPITE the anticipation in Britain surrounding a proposed bout with Frank Bruno, Lennox Lewis had plenty of other options. A host of attractive fights that would have done far more to re-establish Lewis's credibility worldwide were put on the table before the Bruno fight happened. The most financially rewarding of these was a mammoth unification showdown with old Olympic rival Riddick Bowe that would have guaranteed Lewis a minimum of $11m.

Much to Bowe's chagrin, Lewis's camp rejected the offer. The snub left Bowe fuming: 'Lennox Lewis is a pompous, arrogant, phony British punk who is simply afraid to fight me. His cowardly refusal to accept this fight is proof to the world that he is only a pretender to the throne.'

Before this, defences against Tommy Morrison, the new WBO title-holder, and former undisputed champion Evander Holyfield were also mooted. The Morrison fight was put back when the star of *Rocky V* announced he wanted to cash in on the championship he had won against George Foreman with a couple of easy defences before meeting a fighter as dangerous as Lewis.

When Lewis was then offered a defence against Holyfield, that too was rejected. By now, the Lewis camp felt they owed it to the British public to fight Bruno. The late offer to face Bowe in a rematch of their Olympic final would, for many in Lewis's position, have been too hard to resist, but by the time it came in Lewis was already contractually obliged to face Bruno at Cardiff Arms Park on 1 October. If Lewis came through, the plan then was to fight Morrison the following March.

The superbly built Bruno had already challenged twice for the world title, getting stopped in a valiant bid for Tim Witherspoon's WBA crown at Wembley in 1986 before being overpowered by a rusty, out-of-shape Mike Tyson in Las Vegas in 1989. Although one of the hardest punchers in the division and undoubtedly a better boxer than most believed, Bruno had acquired a stigmatic reputation as a gallant loser at the highest level, a fierce competitor let down by questionable stamina and punch resistance.

Out of the ring, Bruno's spontaneous personality and endearing nature had continued to take his appeal beyond boxing's narrow confines and won him wider affection in the hearts of the general public.

Despite his own growing acceptance from the British people, it was an affection Lewis could not come close to matching. This factor added an extra edge to the build-up to what was the first world heavyweight championship fight ever to be staged between two Englishmen. It was also reflected in the mixed reception Lewis received when he got into the ring at close to 1am, with the bout ironically delayed to accommodate the needs of American television. HBO, the cable network, was paying $3.5m for the right to show it live.

In a pre-fight segment, HBO's Jim Lampley said the fight was Britain's equivalent of Ali–Frazier and Leonard–Hearns, and while that may have been an overly flattering comparison there was no denying the enormity and significance of the event.

Colin Hart, the long-serving boxing writer on *The Sun*, Britain's biggest-selling newspaper, said in the same segment: 'There are certain events in the sporting calendar in this country that are considered *national* events. There's Wimbledon tennis fortnight, there's the Royal Ascot race meeting and there's the cup final, which is our equivalent to your [America's] Superbowl. This is on that level.'

With Bruno approaching his 32nd birthday, he was almost four years older than Lewis but he was battle hardened and had lost only to Tyson, Witherspoon and Bonecrusher Smith in 39 fights, with 35 wins inside the distance.

Bruno's experience, and determination, showed from the start. He dictated most of the early rounds behind his ramrod left jab, hurting a below-par Lewis badly in the third with a big right-hander. Lewis's own jab brought up a swelling over Bruno's left eye but it was the challenger who continued to assert himself as the champion struggled to make headway. It wasn't until the sixth that Bruno, hampered by his damaged eye, started to slow down.

In the seventh, with Bruno again forcing the action, Lewis suddenly awoke from his slumber to turn the fight his way. Peppered by a succession of right uppercuts, a wounded Lewis exploded off the ropes with a huge left hook that shook Bruno to his boots. For Bruno, it was a denouement strikingly similar to his 11th-round collapse against Witherspoon. Lewis followed up, unloading from every angle in a desperate bid to finish it. When referee Mickey Vann stepped in, it wasn't, as most thought, to stop the fight but to warn Lewis not to hold and hit.

The interruption was academic. Lewis moved in again and immediately landed a pulverising right uppercut that twisted Bruno's head on his shoulders. After another sickening barrage of blows, a defenceless Bruno, peering submissively out of one eye, was finally rescued. In the space of 30 seconds, Lewis had snatched victory from the jaws of likely defeat – an ability only the greatest champions have.

Although Lewis was still a long way from being able to lay claim to such a grandiose label, he had proved again that he could win when far from his best. 'Lennox Lewis will be a great champion but he still has a lot to learn,' Bruno's brother Michael said in front of the gathered press as the clock ticked deep into the early hours.

Jonathan Rendall of *The Independent* shared the same sentiment, reflecting: 'Maybe this experience will do Lewis some good. The serenity of his image is fine, and arrogance is necessary in a champion. There is no doubt that Lewis did his training but the suspicion is that he regarded Bruno's challenge with a contempt that others would have punished more severely.'

Punishment was coming and it would have serious repercussions. Lewis was now less than a year away from his first crisis but one that would signal the dawn of the most glorious period of his career.

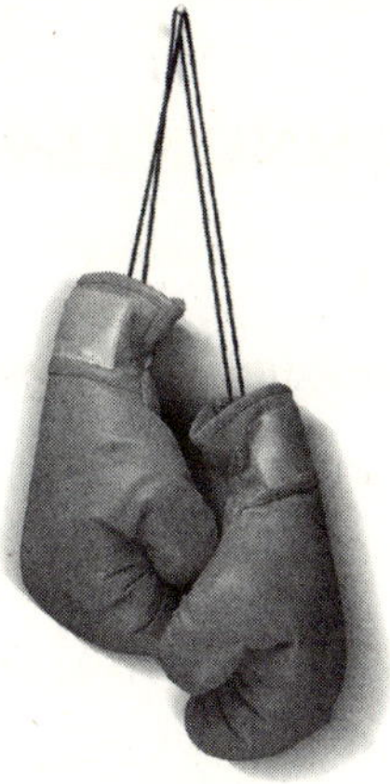

Fight 25

PHIL JACKSON

WBC heavyweight title

Venue: Convention Center, Atlantic City, USA

Date: 6 May 1994

Scheduled rounds: Twelve

Weights: Lewis 235lbs; Jackson 218lbs

Records: Lewis 24-0; Jackson 30-1

Result: Lewis won TKO8

WHEN London-born Michael Bentt travelled to Tulsa, Oklahoma to challenge big-punching Tommy Morrison for his WBO heavyweight title on 29 October 1993, nothing was expected of him. Although a fine amateur who had narrowly missed a place on the American Olympic team in 1988, Bentt had made little progress as a professional. It was expected to be a routine win for Morrison, who was making his second defence of the championship he had won by outboxing George Foreman over 12 rounds in Las Vegas four months earlier.

Boxing, though, is not always so straightforward. Its history is littered with examples of challengers with nothing to lose upsetting champions with nothing to gain. That night, Bentt joined them. Under heavy fire, he rebounded to bomb out Morrison in 93 seconds and send the least credible portion of the world heavyweight title lurching in another unexpected direction.

Bentt's victory had immediate implications for Lennox Lewis. The Briton had been expected to meet Morrison, touted as the next great white hope and with claimed ancestral links to the actor John Wayne, in a big-money match in the spring of 1994. Now he would have to look elsewhere. Not for the first time, Lewis's name was linked with that of Evander Holyfield, who eight days after Lewis's victory over Bruno regained the WBA and IBF versions of the world title by outpointing Riddick Bowe in Las Vegas.

Despite this, it was announced in January that Lewis was likely to make the third defence of his WBC crown against little-known American Phil Jackson in the first week of May. The following month, there was another development when the Lewis camp revealed they had also started negotiations for a title defence in the Philippines, where a proposed bout – although not against Jackson – had the backing of the country's president.

All this speculation was dismissed when Don King began pressing for his fighter, number one contender Oliver McCall, to be the next challenger for Lewis's title. According to WBC rules, all of their world champions must make a mandatory defence at least once a year. King insisted that because Lewis had not actually won his championship in the ring, his bout with Tony Tucker was not a mandatory defence.

The WBC sided with King but it was agreed that Lewis would first make a voluntary defence against Jackson, of Miami, Florida, in Atlantic City on 6 May. If he won, he would make a mandatory defence against McCall immediately afterwards.

Jackson's 30-1 record was impressive on paper but the quality of his opposition did not stand up to close inspection. His only defeat had come against Donovan 'Razor' Ruddock but its manner raised questions about Jackson's character and readiness for a world title challenge. Jackson had been counted out on one knee in the fourth round but his body language suggested he could have continued had he wanted to. Despite the apparent capitulation, Jackson was ranked number five by the WBC and known to be a strong fighter with exceptionally fast hands, although significantly smaller than Lewis.

'Anyone can choke on a given night,' Jackson told the *Baltimore Sun* in reference to the fight that cast serious doubt on whether he could last with Lewis. 'I didn't train properly for Ruddock and had no defense. There was no sense taking a real beating. I knew I'd have another day.'

Jackson's trainer Pat Burns said: 'Put a lot of fighters in that same situation, and they become bums or an opponent. But Phil came back from that fight with a whole new attitude. He busted his butt, and he's won his last five fights. He's done more growing up this past year than he did in his first six years as a pro.

'We've prepared Phil as much mentally as physically. We've got him concentrating on attacking Lewis's body. He's a lot more prepared than when he fought Ruddock. It's strictly how bad he wants to be a champion.'

It wasn't badly enough. Lewis, a 16-1 favourite, completely dominated the fight, landing four times as many punches as Jackson and knocking him down three times on the way to an eighth-round stoppage.

The size difference between the fighters, not to mention the huge gulf in class, played a big part in the outcome. Afterwards, Lewis told the Associated Press: 'I don't mind fighting shorter opponents, because they're going to find it hard to hit me because they have to reach up to hit me. With my reach advantage, it gives them a difficult time.'

Jackson, four inches shorter, sounded as if he was looking for excuses when he said: 'It looks easy on the tape, but when you're standing there looking up at a giant, it's different.'

Lewis's lack of popularity in the US was reflected in the official crowd of 5,534 – only a quarter of the arena's capacity – but he still earned a very respectable $4m compared to Jackson's $500,000. With a well-executed third defence of his title safely completed, Lewis was now ready for McCall.

Or was he?

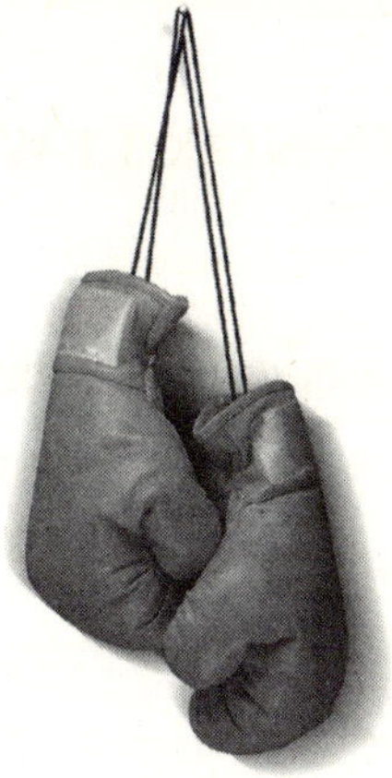

Fight 26

OLIVER McCALL

WBC heavyweight title

Venue: Wembley Arena, London, England

Date: 24 September 1994

Scheduled rounds: Twelve

Weights: Lewis 238lbs; McCall 231¼lbs

Records: Lewis 25-0; McCall 24-5

Result: Lewis LTKO2

WHEN a fighter has a point to prove, no stone is left unturned in his determination to achieve the desired result. He will prepare diligently and invariably reap his reward in the ring. But when he is unmotivated and under-prepared, it is a different story entirely. In with an opponent he perceives as no threat, he places himself in immediate peril.

In Oliver McCall, Lennox Lewis was facing a challenger he did not respect, a man of undoubted physical fortitude but one who was both temperamental and inconsistent. McCall was better known for his countless sparring sessions with Mike Tyson and others than for anything he had achieved in his own career, which had been blighted by drug and alcohol abuse. At 29, McCall had beaten few fighters of note in his 34 bouts and had no championship experience.

Before the fight, Lewis's handlers were busy looking ahead. Frank Maloney, Lewis's manager, had been trying to negotiate a big-money bout with Michael Moorer, the new WBA and IBF champion, before announcing that Lewis would next be defending in a mammoth showdown against bitter rival Riddick Bowe, who had by now been without a championship for nearly a year.

Although McCall was clearly being overlooked, Maloney insisted Lewis's mind was on the job. 'He has this fear of losing, that is one of the greatest things,' Maloney told WireTV. 'If you've got that, you're always going to be on guard and not take any unnecessary chances.'

The rumoured truth appeared to be very different. There were reports that the discordant attitude of trainer Pepe Correa had caused a rift in the camp and affected the usually meticulous Lewis's attitude to training. Lewis had apparently disagreed with the choice of sparring partners brought in and missed parts of his normal routine, sometimes failing to turn up for training at all. It raised concerns over Lewis's physical and mental preparedness for McCall, a fighter he was heavily favoured to beat.

McCall, by contrast, had been training for four months and given himself an extra edge by bringing in a new trainer in the shape of the knowledgeable and respected Emanuel Steward.

Despite the odds against McCall, Steward foresaw his man troubling Lewis. 'Because Lennox is extremely skilful, a good puncher and naturally talented, I think Oliver McCall presents the biggest problem in the world that he could face,' said Steward. 'Oliver's a big, strong man, 230lbs, with tremendous natural reflexes and talent that he has never even utilised. I was amazed when I started working with him at the foot speed that he had in addition to his strength.'

On the night, McCall was the complete antithesis of Lewis. At times, he looked close to the edge mentally, weeping as he walked to the ring while the champion oozed his usual calm. But despite his obvious emotional fragility, the challenger was physically ready and presented a clear and present danger to Lewis.

'I'm gonna be the next heavyweight champion of the world,' McCall had predicted at the press conference to announce the fight a few months earlier. 'Before I come out of the ring, all I'm gonna hear is "the new..."'

Astonishingly, he was right. Twenty seconds into the second round, Lewis's world was turned upside down. As he went to throw a jab, McCall

Olympic super-heavyweight glory for the 22-year-old Lennox Lewis.

Lennox Lewis (left) embarks on his quest for the world heavyweight title with a second-round victory over Al Malcolm at the Royal Albert Hall, London.

The Welshman Andy Gerrard (left) moves to duck under a right hand from Lennox Lewis.

Lennox Lewis (left) attacks the American Michael Epps during his fifth professional outing.

Noel Quarless (left) can't avoid a right hand from the unbeaten Lennox Lewis.

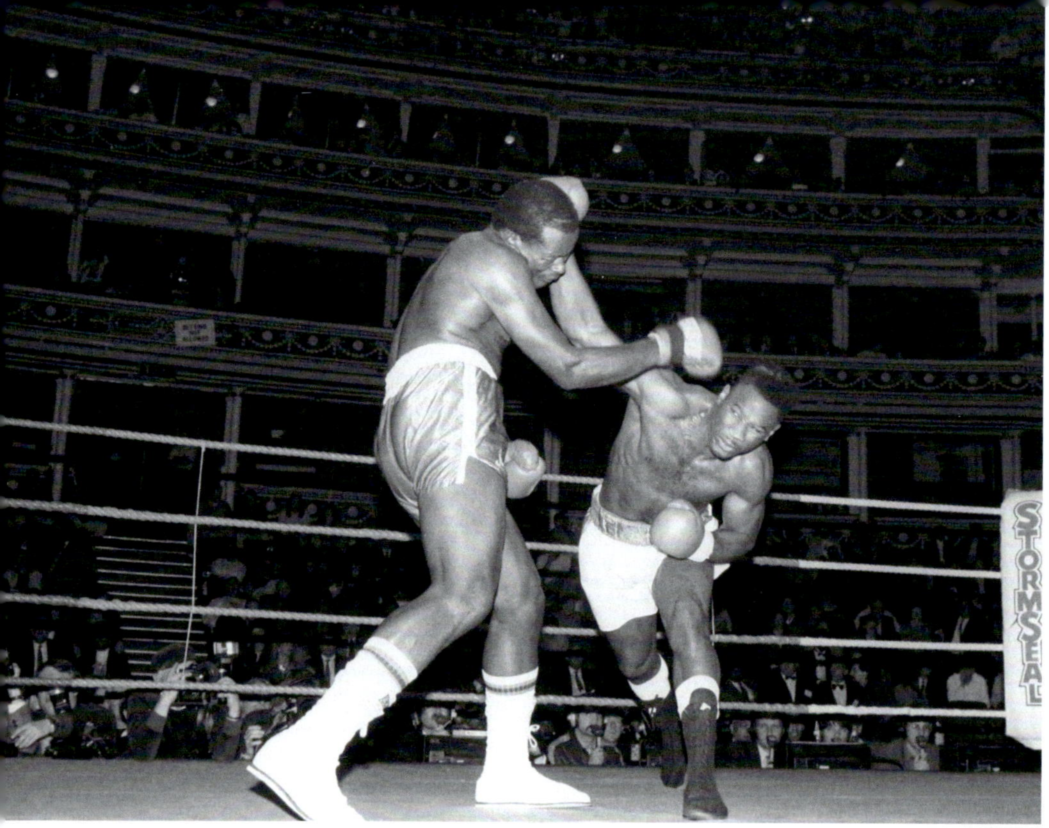

Lennox Lewis (right) lands a long right from out of a crouching position against the African Mike Simuwelu.

The Puerto Rican veteran Ossie Ocasio (right) was definitely a cagey opponent for the young prospect Lennox Lewis.

Lennox Lewis (right) will not be denied as he takes the European crown from the Frenchman Jean-Maurice Chanet.

The previously unbeaten Gary Mason (right) can't keep an accurate Lennox Lewis off during their double-title encounter.

Lennox Lewis (left) gets through with a good left to the head during his quick second-round win over former IBF world cruiserweight champion Glenn McCrory.

Action from the multi-title heavyweight clash between Lennox Lewis (left) and Derek 'Sweet D' Williams at the splendid Royal Albert Hall, London.

It's the end for the dangerous Donovan 'Razor' Ruddock during the second round.

Referee Mickey Vann stops the bout in favour of Lewis (right) during the seventh as Frank Bruno flounders on the ropes.

A facially damaged Justin Fortune is stopped in four by Lennox Lewis.

Lennox Lewis (left) attacks the American Michael Grant during their bout at Madison Square Garden, New York.

The 'White Buffalo' Frans Botha flexes his muscles at the weigh-in for his London encounter with Lennox Lewis.

Lennox Lewis celebrates in familiar fashion as referee Larry O'Connell halts the challenge of Frans Botha.

From left to right Hasim Rahman, complete with crown, promoter Don King, Lennox Lewis's trainer Emanuel Steward and Lewis himself at a pre-fight press conference.

It's a bad day at the office for Lennox Lewis as he suffers a shock devastating loss to the American Hasim Rahman.

A glass screen separates the two men as Lennox Lewis (right) and Hasim Rahman weigh in for their rematch.

A very happy Lewis holds up the belts he regained from Hasim Rahman in Las Vegas, USA.

A confident Lennox Lewis raises his arms aloft after weighing in for the Mike Tyson bout.

A line of security men form a barrier across the ring to separate Mike Tyson (shown) from Lennox Lewis before the start of their Las Vegas encounter.

Lennox Lewis (left) smashes a right hand through the Mike Tyson defence.

An eighth-round end for Mike Tyson at the hands of a dominant Lennox Lewis.

Lennox Lewis and a badly cut Vitali Klitschko exchange blows close to the end of their 2003 encounter.

Lennox Lewis celebrates his eventual sixth-round victory over a brave Vitali Klitschko.

The signs of battle are clearly evident on the face of Vitali Klitschko at the post-fight press conference.

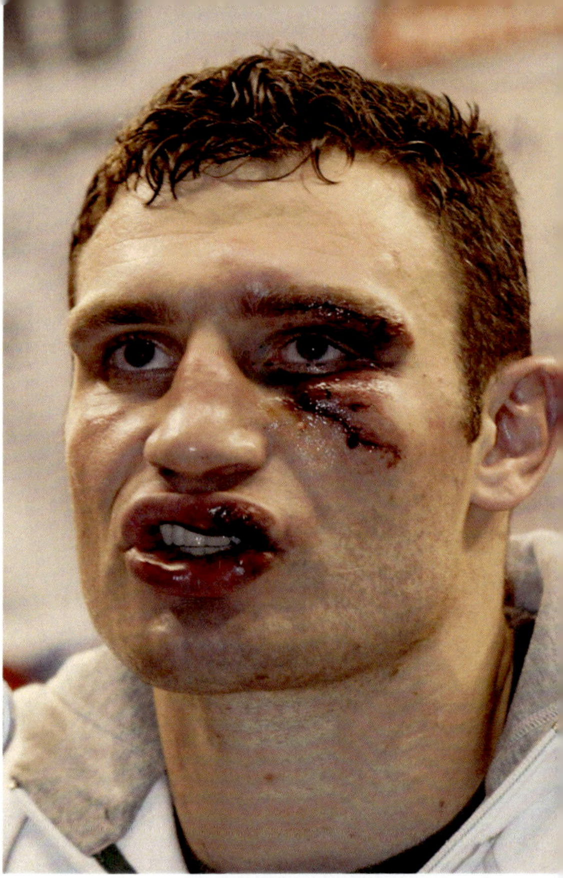

Lennox Lewis (centre) announces his retirement from boxing in London accompanied by his beloved mother Violet (left) and his future wife Violet Chang.

beat him to it with his own right. While Lewis's punch and a following right missed, McCall's found its target, detonating on the point of Lewis's chin. Lewis collapsed instantly on to his back, his face frozen by a vacant glaze. He somehow pulled himself upright but tottered backwards before lurching sideways, almost in the same movement. There was no escaping the crisis. Lewis was gone. Almost instantaneously, as Lewis held up his hands and desperately tried to right himself, referee Jose Garcia waved the fight over. While Lewis, who could barely stand, did his best to look indignant, McCall star-jumped in utter jubilation.

'What can I say?' a tearful McCall told the Associated Press in his dressing room after the fight. 'I am happy, I am thrilled. We knocked him out. We did it!'

In defeat, Lewis was less than gracious, claiming McCall had simply landed a 'lucky punch' and was helped by the referee. His camp later protested but there would be no rematch – at least not yet.

'I am absolutely sure of what I did,' Garcia said later. 'Lennox Lewis was knocked out. To allow more punches to Lennox Lewis would have fatal consequences. My duty is to protect the health of the fighter.'

McCall's victory not only jettisoned Lewis's first reign as champion but also reopened the door to his promoter Don King, who was now awaiting the release from prison of his biggest cash cow, Mike Tyson, with even more relish. Just over a week later, King's re-emergence as a factor in the heavyweight division was greeted memorably in *Sports Illustrated* by the British columnist Hugh McIlvanney.

'It was a night when the most ominous cackle in boxing carried all the way from a northern suburb of London to a cell block in Indiana and sent a shiver down many a spine on both sides of the Atlantic,' McIlvanney wrote. 'Heh, heh, heh, heh, heh. The signature crowing of Don King – even more than the gusher of self-congratulation and mangled quotation it punctuated – let the other leading connivers in the world's most-manipulable sport know exactly what they can expect now that King is back in economic control of the heavyweight division.'

For Lewis, it was the first time in his professional life that he had tasted the pain of defeat. But from every negative comes a positive. He would soon start to rebuild, aided by the very man who had masterminded his downfall – Emanuel Steward.

Emanuel Steward

WITH the writing already on the wall for Pepe Correa before the defeat by Oliver McCall, it was no surprise when Lewis dismissed him. The search to find a suitable replacement began, with the names of Tommy Brooks, George Benton and Emanuel Steward all prominent.

Although Lewis met with George Benton in London and was very impressed with him, he was actually extremely keen on hiring Steward, the man who had masterminded his downfall. After talking to him, Lewis was even more eager to work with Steward. However, Steward was not only expensive but when he worked with a fighter on a long-term basis he also liked to have a role in the management side as well. Due to this, Lewis's handlers were naturally not as keen on the American as Lennox was.

Eventually, and somewhat reluctantly, Lewis agreed to go for another American in the form of Thell Torrence and a deal with him was struck. But Lewis remained resolute in his convictions and the deal was subsequently scrapped. On 27 January 1995, Lewis's handlers agreed to a long-term deal with Steward, which included a manager's role. But in taking up the position, Steward was himself giving up things that could have been beneficial to him financially, mainly his association with Don King. This, of course, meant him leaving his role with McCall and forfeiting the opportunity of working with Mike Tyson on his eventual release from prison. Despite this, Steward had openly stated he considered Lewis to be the best heavyweight out there.

Born the son of a coalminer in Bottom Creek, West Virginia, on 7 July 1944, Steward moved to Detroit with his mother at the age of 12, where he started boxing at the Brewster Recreational Center, world-renowned as the place where the legendary Joe Louis honed his skills. He eventually went on to amass a tremendous amateur tally of 98 fights with only three losses, a record that saw him become the 1963 bantamweight National Golden Gloves champion at the age of only 18. Even though the natural progression for Steward would have been to turn professional, he could not find a management package that suited his needs and instead took a job as an electrician with the Detroit Edison Company.

However, he never lost his love of boxing. In 1971, he took his half-brother James to a local gymnasium to show him a few moves. The gym in question was a rather drab-looking one situated in the basement of a recreation centre on the near south-east side of Detroit. As he continued to attend, he used the knowledge he had from his own amateur days to get himself involved with the training programme there. Soon, he became a part-time coach at what was known as the Kronk boxing team and with his help they went on to win the 1971 Detroit Golden Gloves competition.

In March 1972, Steward then became the full-time trainer and manager at the Kronk gym. After turning his attentions to professional boxing, his first world champion was crowned on 2 March 1980 courtesy of the lightweight Hilmer Kenty, who successfully relieved the Venezuelan Ernesto Espana of his WBA title by a ninth-round stoppage.

Since then, Steward had gone on to work with numerous top-ranked and world championship-level fighters, including the legendary Thomas 'Hitman' Hearns. Of particular interest to Lewis was that he had been instrumental in helping Evander Holyfield secure an unexpected points victory over Riddick Bowe in November 1993, as well as McCall's unhinging of Lewis himself. It was hoped that he would be able to use his vast knowledge and knowhow to get Lewis's career back on track as soon as possible.

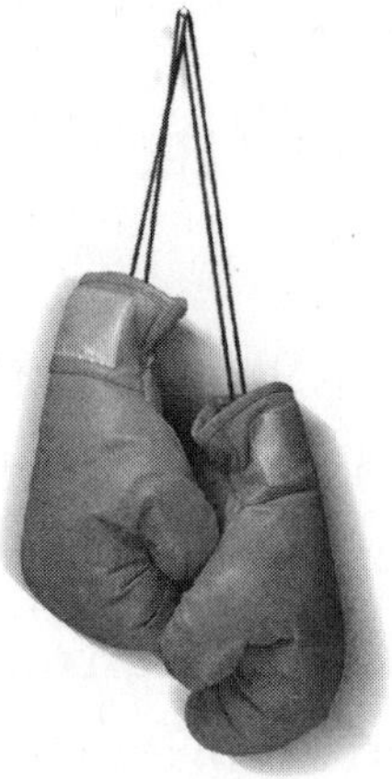

Fight 27

LIONEL BUTLER

WBC heavyweight title final eliminator

Venue: Arco Arena, Sacramento, California, USA

Date: 13 May 1995

Scheduled rounds: Twelve

Weights: Lewis 248lbs; Butler 261lbs

Records: Lewis 25-1; Butler 22-10-1

Result: Lewis won TKO5

DESPITE the expectation of a Don King-orchestrated WBC shut-out, the organisation still had Lennox Lewis at number three, behind Tony Tucker and Lionel Butler, just over a month after the defeat by Oliver McCall. They decreed that Lewis should meet the highest available contender in a final eliminator for its title.

At the end of 1994, it was decided that Lewis would face Butler, a King fighter, in Las Vegas on 18 March 1995. The bout was due to be part of a triple-header of former world heavyweight champions that would also feature Michael Moorer and Evander Holyfield, but when Holyfield withdrew from his proposed fight against South African Corrie Sanders the show was cancelled.

A problem involving Butler then arose, putting the bout with Lewis in jeopardy. Fearing Butler would drop out, Lewis's manager Frank Maloney called for his man to be allowed to meet the next highest available contender in the final eliminator instead. Butler's issues were drug related and he had also allegedly signed conflicting contracts with different promoters.

Eventually, Butler confirmed he was fit and available to fight. The WBC put the fight out to purse bids and despite several venues and dates being mentioned it was announced that Lewis would meet Butler at the Arco Arena in Sacramento, California on 13 May.

Although erratic, Butler was a dangerous opponent for Lewis at such a crucial point in his career. Short for a heavyweight at just 5ft 11in, he was extremely powerful, particularly with the left hook. Butler had knocked out former champions Tony Tubbs and James 'Bonecrusher' Smith but had a patchy record, with ten defeats in 33 fights by the time he met Lewis. One of those had come against Riddick Bowe, who at the time was making his professional debut.

An added twist saw Pepe Correa, the trainer Lewis had fired, brought in to help Butler. 'Lucifer, I'm telling you it's Lucifer,' Correa told Michael Katz of the *New York Daily News* before the bout. 'You think Oliver McCall is crazy? This guy is awesome. I'm working with Lucifer – and he's a hell of a fighter.'

Stung by the nature of the McCall defeat, and not wanting to risk a repeat, Lewis had prepared thoroughly under new trainer Emanuel Steward at the Kronk gym in Detroit and then at Big Bear in California. Although he came in at 248lbs, the heaviest weight of his career, Lewis looked lean and strong. Butler, by contrast, was dreadfully out of condition.

After a few nervy moments and a string of warnings for pushing Butler, Lewis finally closed the show. With the crowd booing, he floored Butler for a second time at the end of the fifth round before the fight was stopped. Butler finished in a sitting position, enmeshed in the ropes and cowering away from Lewis's final right hand.

The victory lifted Lewis into the mandatory challenger's spot with the WBC but his position was only notional. The WBC had already promised to install Tyson as its number one contender before his release from prison, which meant that Lewis was behind him in the pecking order.

Nonetheless, Steward declared himself satisfied with Lewis's performance after their first fight together. 'Lennox could have taken Butler out earlier but I didn't want him to take any chances,' Steward said. 'I wanted Lennox to concentrate on zones he could control from the outside.'

King was predictably unimpressed with the victor, telling the media: 'Lewis had nothing to beat but he didn't give value for money. It was exactly the sort of fight that's driving people away from boxing. Most of the time he ran away. Can you imagine what Tyson would have done to Butler? It would have been all over in a round. It's only a matter of time before Tyson mows all of them down.'

Ken Jones, the veteran British scribe, who was ringside for *The Independent*, was also critical of Lewis, reporting: 'If there was merit in Lewis's performance, the inescapable conclusion is that he remains more of an athlete than a natural fighter. At 29, he is not old for a heavyweight but he may have passed the age of improvement.'

Jones was wrong. Lewis would improve immeasurably and his greatest nights were still to come.

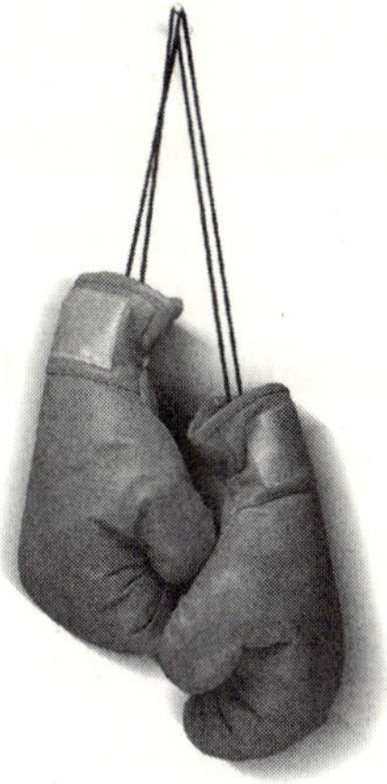

Fight 28

JUSTIN FORTUNE

Venue: The Point, Dublin, Ireland

Date: 2 July 1995

Scheduled rounds: Twelve

Weights: Lewis 246lbs; Fortune 216lbs

Records: Lewis 26-1; Fortune 11-2-1

Result: Lewis won TKO4

AUSTRALIA has never been a hotbed for heavyweights, so Justin Fortune had nothing to live up to when he agreed to face Lennox Lewis at The Point Theatre, in Dublin, seven weeks after the Lionel Butler fight. Fortune had only had 14 fights, the most notable of which was an eighth-round stoppage loss to Buster Mathis Jr, who would lose to Mike Tyson five months later.

But although he lacked experience, Fortune brought toughness and a fearless mentality into his fight with Lewis, who was marking time while he built towards what he hoped was another championship fight.

At only 5ft 8in, Fortune was built along Tyson lines and gave away nine inches in height to Lewis. The gulf in size and class was always likely to prove unbridgeable, but it didn't stop the plucky Australian preparing with almost manic intensity.

It was witnessed first hand by John Wight of the *Morning Star*, London, who later recalled the experience of watching Fortune prepare at legendary trainer Freddie Roach's Outlaws gym in Los Angeles.

'Justin himself was working like a madman on one of the heavy bags,' Wight wrote in a comment piece entitled 'Justin Fortune's Shot At The Big Time', published nearly 20 years later. 'The fight was scheduled to take place in six weeks, which meant there was no time to waste. This was his shot and he knew it. So did Freddie.

'Watching Justin spar in the days and weeks following was frightening. He was not a guy who believed in taking it easy or holding back in sparring, as some fighters preferred to. As he told me one day, "There's no friends in the ring."

I remember watching him spar this young kid who'd just turned pro. His trainer felt that sparring Justin would help the young lad's development. Within two rounds, the kid's body had taken such a pounding it had to be stopped.

'It was the same story with other sparring partners brave enough to share the ring with Justin and Freddie was worried – at this rate his fighter would run out of people to work with.

'Freddie managed to secure the services of former heavyweight champ Tony Tubbs to spar with Justin.

'There was only two weeks left of serious training by this point and Justin was mean, lean and focused. Tony Tubbs, by contrast, turned up at the gym 15 minutes late looking as if he'd come straight from the McDonald's up the street.

'He was smiling and relaxed and he looked like he'd never trained in his life. With him was his wife and trainer, an old guy who walked with a limp.

'Waiting for him to get ready, Justin paced around the gym mumbling expletives under his breath as he grew angrier by the second. Another 15 minutes passed before Tubbs was ready to step into the ring to start sparring. I was certain he was going to be massacred.

'The buzzer went and instantly Justin moved in and started letting his hands go. Tubbs took every one of his shots on the shoulders and arms, before countering with a couple of short inside uppercuts to send Justin staggering back a few steps. Justin regrouped and came back with another combination.

'This time Tubbs shuffled a couple of quick steps to his right and caught him with a left hook to the head and a right uppercut to the body.

'I couldn't believe what I was seeing. By the end of the first round Justin was out of ideas, his confidence shattered against a fat but more skilled opponent. Freddie brought the workout to an end after one more round. It did not bode well.'

Indeed it didn't. Predictably, Lewis proved too much. Fortune, who had most of the 3,000-strong crowd behind him, fought valiantly and even made the former champion wince with a body shot in the first round. But despite his constant bobbing and weaving, Fortune couldn't get close enough to do any more damage. In the fourth, three successive right uppercuts staggered Fortune and sent him down. Although he got straight back up, a reaction that typified the underdog's defiance, the fight was stopped.

Lewis paid tribute to Fortune afterwards, telling Gary Norman of Sky Sports: 'He was very game. He threw some good punches. I hit him with some tremendous shots and it was surprising that he didn't go down [earlier], but

I knew the uppercuts would get to him. I was a bit cautious in the first round then Manny [Emanuel Steward] told me to step it up, so I did. He actually caught me in the first round with a good shot and that kinda woke me up, so I started [landing] my punches.'

In the grand scheme of things, Lewis's victory over Fortune was meaningless, little more than a glorified gym workout. His next assignment, though, promised to make considerably more impact.

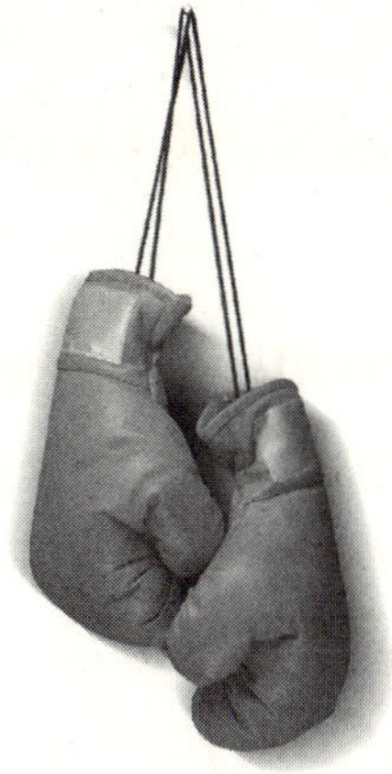

Fight 29

TOMMY MORRISON

Venue: Convention Center, Atlantic City, USA

Date: 7 October 1995

Scheduled rounds: Twelve

Weights: Lewis 241lbs; Morrison 227lbs

Records: Lewis 27-1; Morrison 45-2-1

Result: Lewis won TKO6

TOMMY Morrison was a compelling figure long before he finally climbed into the ring to fight Lennox Lewis in Atlantic City towards the end of 1995. Forced to leave school early in order to support his family financially, Morrison entered tough man competitions at 13, winning fights against grown men. He turned professional at 19 and was a Hollywood film star by the age of 21 after landing the role of Tommy Gunn, Sylvester Stallone's protege, in *Rocky V.*

With his early promise clear, boxing's obsession with racial distinctions inevitably led to Morrison being labelled America's next Great White Hope, a burdensome tag previously worn by Gerry Cooney. To enrich the narrative, Morrison was also promoted as the great nephew of John Wayne – real name Marion Morrison – the legendary American actor and star of countless Westerns.

Morrison's charisma and concussive punching power, particularly with the left hook, quickly turned him into an attraction but, like Cooney, he was vulnerable himself. After steaming through his first 28 opponents,

Morrison was sickeningly knocked out in the fifth round by Ray Mercer, the same fighter who had denied him a spot at the 1988 Olympics. Morrison bounced back to outbox George Foreman for the vacant WBO title in June 1993 but just when a fight against Lewis looked imminent Morrison imploded again, getting stopped in less than a round by huge outsider Michael Bentt in his second defence.

When the fight with Lewis eventually happened, it was 18 months later and under entirely different circumstances, with neither holding titles or receiving anything like the purses originally on offer. Although his victory over Lionel Butler had earned Lewis the WBC mandatory challenger's position on paper, new champion Frank Bruno was lining up a first defence against Mike Tyson, who had been installed as the number one contender on his release from prison. Lewis had to win just to stay where he was and Morrison could ill afford another defeat.

Before the bout, Lewis's manager Frank Maloney told Michael Katz of the *New York Daily News* that the loser 'may as well walk on to the beach and straight out into the ocean, because there's nowhere else to go'.

Morrison's trainer Tom Virgets spelt out his man's tactics, admitting: 'Because Tommy is so much shorter, there is no future in trying to fight Lewis from the outside. He'd just be soaking up the jab. He's got to stay low and fight from a crouch, come in under Lewis's arms and throw combinations.

'According to the level of Tommy's hips, he goes from being an exceptional fighter to less than mediocre. From a crouch, he does terrible damage to the body and is in position to deliver big head punches, especially with his left. If he forgets to stay low, then I'm afraid Lewis will murder him.'

Lewis's trainer Emanuel Steward said: 'Lennox doesn't have to worry about the other guy's style. He's got all the power and speed to take fights away from his opponents. There isn't a problem he can't handle. Tommy's dangerous but Lennox will get rid of him quickly, no more than three rounds.'

Steward was wrong but not by much. Morrison lasted into the sixth. Like many previous opponents, he couldn't find a way past Lewis's jab and was dominated from the start. Lewis used his left hand to great effect to floor Morrison three times, with the loser finishing cut around both eyes and thoroughly demoralised.

'I nullified his left hook,' Lewis said in a report published in the *Los Angeles Times* after the fight. 'I [have] got an arsenal filled with punches. The best of Lennox Lewis is yet to come. Put the right opponent in front of me and different things come out.'

Despite the one-sided nature of the fight, Lewis failed to win Morrison's respect. 'I never was impressed with Lennox Lewis,' Morrison told Mark Workman of *boxingscene.com* a few months after the bout. 'I didn't think he hit hard worth a crap. He had no power. I didn't think so. I'd never been more confident for a fight in my life. I figured I'd blow him out in three rounds. Lennox Lewis fights scared.'

In February 1996, Morrison was diagnosed HIV positive and spent years trying to disprove the initial test results. After a ten-year retirement, he came back and won two fights against nondescript opposition. In 2013, Morrison died from multiple organ failure aged just 44. Reports said he had been suffering with full-blown AIDS and bedridden for over a year.

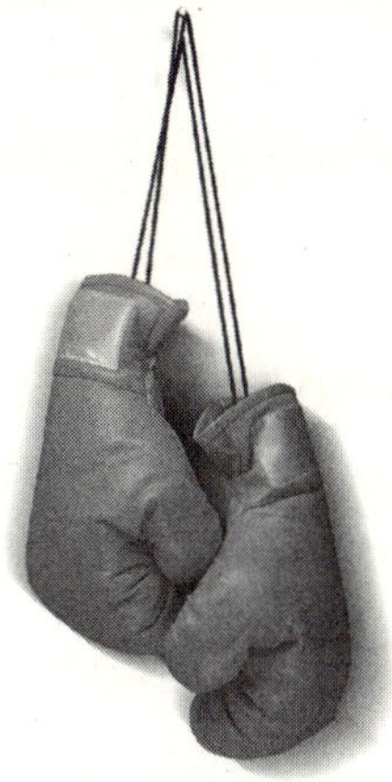

Fight 30

RAY MERCER

Venue: Madison Square Garden, New York, USA

Date: 10 May 1996

Scheduled distance: Ten rounds

Weights: Lewis 247lbs; Mercer 238lbs

Records: Lewis 28-1; Mercer 23-3-1

Result: Lewis won pts 10

AFTER failing in a legal bid to stop Frank Bruno defending the WBC title against Mike Tyson, who would quickly and conclusively regain the championship he first won a decade earlier, Lennox Lewis was initially lined up to challenge old rival Riddick Bowe for the WBO crown in Las Vegas on 20 April 1996. Bowe then changed his mind and decided to face the Pole Andrew Golota instead. As a result, in early February, it was announced that Lewis's next opponent would be the former world champion Ray Mercer in New York on 10 May.

Mercer, a teak-tough former army sergeant, had captured the heavyweight gold medal at the 1988 Seoul Olympics, where Lewis had beaten Riddick Bowe to win the super-heavyweight title. They turned professional on separate but parallel tracks but Mercer became a world champion first, winning the lesser-regarded WBO title with a ninth-round KO of the Italian Francesco Damiani, who had outboxed him for most of the fight.

Mercer then retained his championship with a dramatic destruction of rising star

Tommy Morrison but was somewhat exposed in his next fight when losing on points to the veteran former champion Larry Holmes. By the time he fought Lewis, Mercer had been out of the ring for nearly a year, losing a unanimous decision in his previous bout to Evander Holyfield after a punishing battle in which he was knocked down for the first time in his career in the eighth round.

In the build-up to the fight with Mercer, Lewis's trainer Emanuel Steward talked about his flourishing relationship with his charge, telling HBO: 'I believe that the chemistry between Lennox and I is going to make a big difference and that's something that's so important. I felt that he needed a really strong person that he could respect. He's a strong-minded individual himself.'

Steward said one of the things that impressed him most about Lewis was his 'willingness to learn, change and accept his weak points', adding: 'I always discuss things with him. He's an exceptionally intelligent person and he and I are mentally on the same wavelength.'

It was just as well. The fight with Mercer turned out to be the hardest of Lewis's career to date. Lewis gave as good as he got but was backed up and hurt a number of times by the aggressive Mercer.

After ten rounds, both fighters were heavily marked and bleeding from their mouths, but Lewis had done just enough in the eyes of the judges. He was awarded a majority decision, winning by a single point on one card, two points on the second while the third judge scored the fight a draw. The crowd of nearly 18,000 booed the decision, with many believing Mercer had won the fight.

'I hit him with some shots and he kept coming,' Lewis told the Associated Press after the fight. 'Ray Mercer gave me a lot of pressure. This was a positive step toward a [Mike] Tyson fight. I'm not taking any easy fights. This was preparation for a Mike Tyson fight.'

Steward defended Lewis's showing. 'Lennox hasn't been in this type of fight before,' he told Alan Goldstein of the *Baltimore Sun*. 'Normally, when a British fighter gets in a slugfest like this, he caves in. It may not have been a great performance, but he gutted it out and raised himself another level.'

Out of the ring, Lewis had already won a court judge's backing in his fight to ensure Tyson defended against him first, but he clearly wanted to settle their differences in the ring.

'I don't want to beat Tyson in the court, I want to win in the ring,' Lewis told the same newspaper. 'Maybe Tyson will have the guts to tell [Don] King he's not giving up his title without a fight. If I never get to fight Tyson, it will be his shame, not mine.'

The fight would happen but not for another six years, by which time Lewis had almost reached the end of the road.

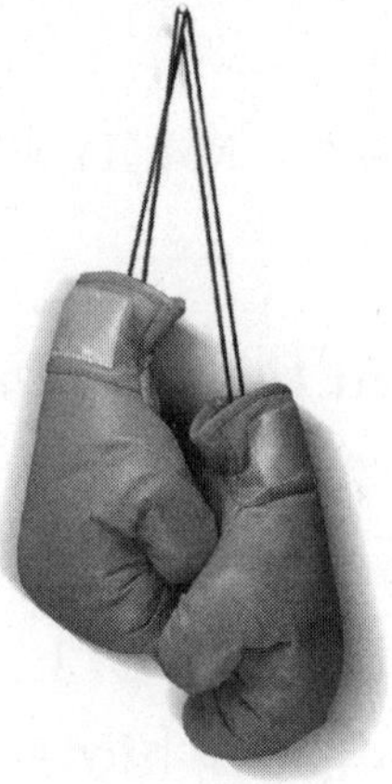

Fight 31

OLIVER McCALL II

Vacant WBC heavyweight title

Venue: Las Vegas Hilton, Las Vegas, USA

Date: 7 February 1997

Scheduled distance: Twelve rounds

Weights: Lewis 251lbs; McCall 237lbs

Records: Lewis 29-1; McCall 28-6

Result: Lewis won TKO5

AFTER more than two years in the boxing wilderness, the waiting was finally over. Lennox Lewis was getting his shot at redemption, a chance to reclaim the championship he had lost so violently and controversially in London. When it came, the man in the opposite corner was not Mike Tyson, who had been compelled by a court to face him, but Oliver McCall, the very fighter who had ended Lewis's first reign in such stunning fashion. The fight came about because the Tyson camp had gone back on an agreement to face Lewis in a mandatory defence of the WBC title and vacated, having previously paid Lewis $4m in step-aside money to allow Tyson to fight Bruce Seldon for the WBA title.

Despite his disappointment at not facing Tyson – at least not yet – the outcome was poetic for Lewis. He now had the chance to put the record straight against McCall and do it as a much-improved fighter. There would be no underestimating his opponent this time. Lewis had spent $250,000 preparing at a training camp in Scottsdale, Arizona and pushed himself hard. He did not intend to fail.

'If he beats me this time, I'll retire,' Lewis told Dean Juipe of the *Las Vegas Sun* before the bout. 'I'm pretty sure he won't. I realise I made a mistake.'

Emanuel Steward, who had led McCall to victory in the first fight before switching camps, said: 'When I got Lennox, I think he was performing at about 40 per cent of his ability or potential. Now I'd say he's at about 70 per cent. He's got to win impressively. He wasn't impressive in their first fight. But my job is to bring out the best that Lennox has, and if I do that it should bring him a victory.'

Lewis added: 'My chin was out and exposed [in the first fight] and he clipped it. It won't happen again. I'm with a great trainer, I'm mentally tougher than I ever was and I'm physically more aware. I don't think I'll ever look bad again.

'I'll say this: I'm prepared for a long fight. I don't think he can outbox me and it would be fine with me if he comes out and comes right at me.

'It's taken me two years to get into this position. I'm not going to mess it up.'

Despite his continuing rehabilitation for drug and alcohol abuse and increasingly unpredictable behaviour, McCall sounded confident. 'I'm clean and sober. I have the eye of the tiger for Lewis. Drugs and alcohol is a disease, but I'm responsible for my recoveries. I don't have any excuses. I'm living day by day. I am in the same shape as when I knocked Lewis out first time. I'm like Clark Kent. I want to be Superman again. I have people taking care of my legal matters and I'm ready to fight.'

He wasn't. After a competitive first two rounds, McCall went into meltdown. It led to one of the strangest endings to a fight in boxing history. By the end of the fourth, by which time he had stopped fighting completely, McCall was in tears in his corner. Referee Mills Lane spoke to him for a second time and McCall was allowed to come out for the fifth, but when his odd demeanour continued Lane stopped the fight, giving Lewis the vacant title but not the sort of redemption he had sought.

The next day, McCall tried to explain away what had resembled an emotional breakdown. 'My strategy was – and I know it sounds kind of absurd – was a kind of rope-a-dope,' he told a news conference, reported in the *New York Times*. 'I didn't quit, I came to win.' Later McCall, whose $3m purse was suspended, called for a rematch, insisting: 'All of my proceeds will be given to charity. I don't want the money. Not only do I want a rematch, I'll knock Lewis out.'

Astonishingly, psychiatrist Dr Leonora Petty, who examined McCall, told the media: 'I think his mental state is just fine.'

In an interview published in *The Guardian* 12 years later, Lewis's manager Frank Maloney recalled one of boxing's oddest nights.

'What we saw that night wasn't a fight, it was a grown man having a breakdown in the ring. I couldn't believe what I was seeing – we'd seen him in the build-up, at the press conferences, walking around the hotel, and he was fine. I hadn't heard that anything was wrong.

'We realised, though, after the fight, that we'd witnessed a man break down. Our celebrations weren't anywhere near what we'd normally have. I think it was quite muted.

'You know, in Vegas, nothing surprises you. You can always expect the unexpected in Vegas, but I must say that was one of the more bizarre fights I've ever been involved in.'

Bizarre or not, Lewis had regained what he lost and was about to embark on the most prolific period of his career.

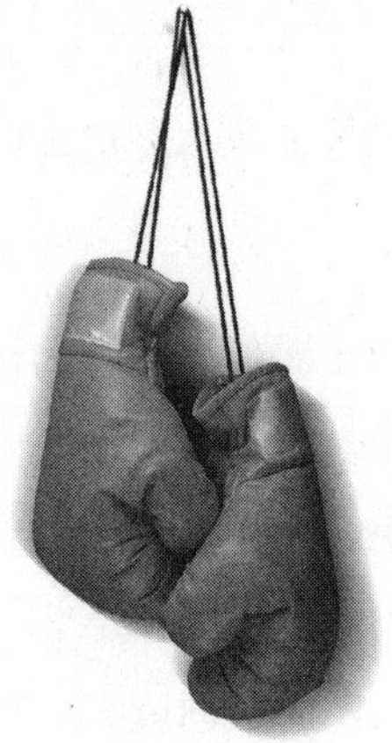

Fight 32

HENRY AKINWANDE

WBC heavyweight title

Venue: Caesars Palace, Lake Tahoe, USA

Date: 12 July 1997

Scheduled distance: Twelve rounds

Weights: Lewis 242lbs; Akinwande 237½lbs

Records: Lewis 30-1; Akinwande 32-0-1

Result: Lewis won DQ5

AFTER his tainted victory over Oliver McCall, Lennox Lewis was initially ordered to defend his newly regained WBC title within 90 days against Henry Akinwande, a British-born heavyweight with parental roots in Nigeria. Akinwande, another fighter controlled by Don King, had relinquished the WBO title in order to maintain his number three ranking with the WBC.

Out of the ring, Lewis had been basking in the limelight since his win over McCall. On 18 March, he unveiled a mural of himself at Babe Ruth's London Docklands restaurant to cap a week of awards. He had also been honoured in the House of Commons and presented with a plaque by the Lonsdale Club for becoming the first British fighter to regain the world heavyweight title.

With the Akinwande fight looming, Lewis took an early swipe at the challenger's credentials, bragging: 'He may be bigger than me but he's definitely not stronger – and he doesn't have my will. I get the feeling that all he has is his jab. He will find I'm in a different league.'

After the deadline for purse bids was put back four times, Lewis's handlers Panos Eliades and New Jersey-based Main Events reached agreement with King for the bout to take place at the Convention Center, Atlantic City on 12 July. However, because King was disqualified from working in New Jersey owing to a tax fraud indictment, the fight was moved to the Maximus Theater at Caesars Palace, Lake Tahoe, where Lewis had already beaten Mike Weaver in July 1991.

With the disgraceful ear-biting incident that had marred the rematch between Mike Tyson and Evander Holyfield two weeks earlier still fresh in the memory, the heavyweight division needed a lift. But because Lewis and Akinwande were both British, interest in the US was limited. The bout was held in a very small arena and the fighters only shared a purse of around $3m, a fraction of what Tyson and Holyfield received (although Tyson's purse was subsequently withheld).

Despite this, the fight looked competitive on paper, with both men statistically well matched. At 31, they were the same age and there was only a couple of inches between them in height, with Akinwande the taller at 6ft 7in. The fighters also had similar professional records. While Lewis was the betting favourite, there were many who thought Akinwande, a former European and Commonwealth champion, had the style to cause him problems. He did – but the problems were not of a conventional nature. For most of the five rounds the fight lasted, Akinwande clung to Lewis like a drowning sailor clinging to a mast. Unable to compete physically, the challenger quickly went into survival mode. After an appalling spectacle punctuated by repeated warnings and a point deduction for holding, referee Mills Lane finally lost patience with Akinwande and disqualified him.

Lewis snapped afterwards: 'I said from the beginning that Akinwande was going to get hammered. He elected to hold and what can I do? I'll fight anybody. George Foreman, Evander Holyfield, anybody they put in front of me. I have never ducked anybody, but everybody keeps ducking me. I want to unify the title.'

An unrepentant Akinwande clearly saw another fight, telling the media at the post-fight press conference: 'I don't think I did that much holding. I tried to work my jab, but he stopped me from working inside. I put Lewis down in the third round but the referee didn't count it. I don't think the referee should have stopped the fight.'

Glyn Leach, who was ringside for *The Independent*, wrote: 'The only thing pretty about this fight was the setting – Lake Tahoe, a scenic, waterside ski resort in the mountains on the Nevada–California border. Intimidated by the power and strength of the champion, Akinwande clung on for dear life wherever possible, ruining the contest as a spectacle. For the fourth time in 12 months, a major heavyweight fight ended with a disqualification ... now boxing has incurred another stain that seems unlikely to come out in the wash.'

Once again, and through no fault of his own, a Lewis victory had been soured by the behaviour of his opponent. What Lewis really needed was a chance to make a clear, conclusive statement against a credible challenger. He would get it in his next fight – and take it with both hands.

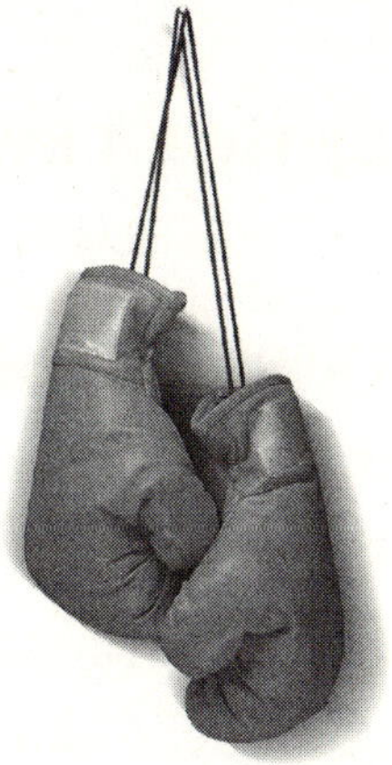

Fight 33

ANDREW GOLOTA

WBC heavyweight title

Venue: Convention Center, Atlantic City, USA

Date: 4 October 1997

Scheduled distance: Twelve rounds

Weights: Lewis 244lbs; Golota 244lbs

Records: Lewis 31-1; Golota 28-2

Result: Lewis won TKO1

DESPITE twice appearing to suffer some sort of psychological malfunction in his two losses to Riddick Bowe, leading to back-to-back disqualifications, there was no doubting that Andrew Golota was a talented and marketable heavyweight. The Chicago-based Pole had given Bowe hell in both bouts, in which he was ahead on points before being thrown out for blatant low blows. Although the transgressions were construed by some as a symptom of deeper mental fragility under pressure, Golota had shown enough ability to warrant a championship chance. Lewis needed a high-profile challenger and despite suggestions the job might go to the Dane Brian Nielsen, it was Golota who got the call, largely at the behest of HBO, the cable TV network that had screened most of Lewis's fights in America.

After the frustration of his last two fights, Lewis now had a chance to look explosive against an opponent who would come straight to him. There was also an opportunity to better the performances of Bowe, his bitter rival, who had struggled to subdue Golota in both their bouts and taken heavy punishment in the process, going down twice legitimately in the second fight. The Lewis–Golota bout was to be screened live in Poland in a semi-permanent tent situated in the capital city of Warsaw, so becoming the first-ever sporting event to be televised live to a paying audience in that country. The fight was also Lewis's first pay-per-view event to be aired in the US.

Bad blood flowed before the gloves were even donned. Golota refused to take part in a conference call eight days before the bout after objecting to suggestions by Lewis's manager Frank Maloney that he had been taking steroids.

'This is the same accusation that was made before the Bowe fight,' Golota's trainer Roger Bloodworth said in a report published in the *New York Times*. 'We took a test. No steroids. It's a Maloney smokescreen. They're just trying to build up their fighter's confidence. We've been down the steroids test route. It's no big deal.'

Lewis said: 'The only comment I can make is whatever vitamins he's taking is giving him a chemical imbalance. It's caused him to lose his mind in the ring. I hope he sorts out the problem before he gets in the ring. Whatever it is, I don't think it will get his chin any stronger.' Bloodworth promised there would be no repeat of the blatant low blows that had seen Golota, previously unbeaten in 28 bouts, disqualified twice against Bowe in consecutive fights in July and December 1996. 'We've straightened him out,' Bloodworth said. 'You've got my guarantee there won't be any low blows.'

Lewis's trainer Emanuel Steward was less convinced. 'I'm not confident he will fight properly,' Steward said in a report in the *Irish Times*. 'He cannot control what he does. Whenever he is in any sort of distress, he resorts to dirty tactics. There is a good possibility he will snap, throw low blows and throw the fight.

'The only thing I am concerned about is that Lennox gets out there and imposes himself immediately. I don't believe Golota will stand up once he gets hit on the chin. Lennox should be too big and too strong and I believe he will win by knockout – but only if he fights his fight.'

He did. It lasted 95 seconds, with Lewis delivering arguably the single most devastating performance of his career. Golota was down, wide-eyed in shock, inside the first minute and destroyed within seconds of getting up as Lewis moved in on him like a cold-blooded assassin. His chest-thumping celebration said it all: 'Challenge me if you dare.'

Lewis said after the fight: 'I wanted to get rid of all the misfits and this was the last misfit. I wanted to make my statement. I wanted to consolidate all the belts and be one of the best heavyweights in the world. I wanted to knock him out before he had any chance to commit any fouls. I wasn't worried about what he was going to do. I just had to do my job and hit him.'

Golota, who said the pressure of the fight had caused him to freeze, was later taken to hospital after collapsing in his dressing room but made a full recovery.

Richard Hoffer wrote in *Sports Illustrated*: 'In a late effort to restore some gloss to his career, Lewis gave just the kind of performance that, if it didn't legitimize his sport, nudged it back toward normalcy. He was in the ring just one minute and 35 seconds and threw only 36 punches, but in that brief showing he proved he was worthy of a heavyweight championship and that the division still had life in it.'

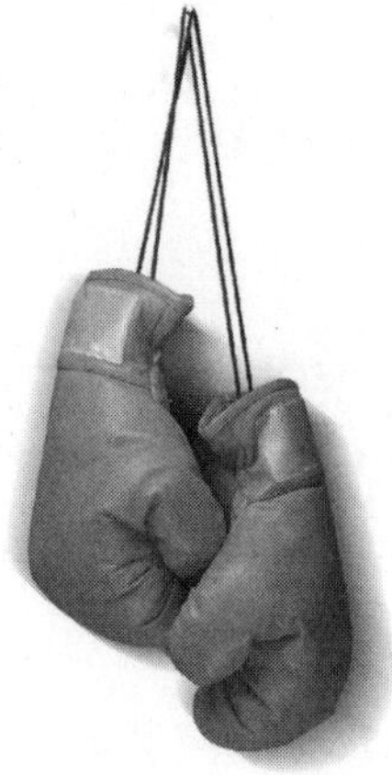

Fight 34

SHANNON BRIGGS

WBC heavyweight title

Venue: Convention Center, Atlantic City, USA

Date: 28 March 1998

Scheduled distance: Twelve rounds

Weights: Lewis 243lbs; Briggs 228lbs

Records: Lewis 32-1; Briggs 30-1

Result: Lewis won TKO5

SEVERAL days after his sensational victory over Andrew Golota, Lennox Lewis was offered $20m to meet his old rival Ray Mercer in a rematch. Mercer even said he would be willing to fight for free if Lewis also donated $10m to charity if he lost. There was another option too. Former undisputed world champion James 'Buster' Douglas, the first man to beat Mike Tyson, was also suggested as a possible opponent for Lewis. Frank Maloney, Lewis's manager, said: 'I think Douglas is a good fight as there is still mystique about him.' Douglas declared: 'I am ready to take on Lennox Lewis. His opponents don't stand up to him but I will, baby!'

Meanwhile, Lewis turned up at the Thomas & Mack Center in Las Vegas to watch the WBA and IBF title unification bout between Evander Holyfield and Michael Moorer. He hoped to secure a three-title match with the winner. Holyfield, who had lost on points to Moorer over 12 rounds in April 1994, gained revenge when he stopped Moorer at the end of the eighth round. Moorer was knocked down five times. Afterwards, Holyfield said he would be willing to face Lewis if a deal could be made.

After a series of negotiations, it was announced that a deal had been struck between Lewis's handlers and Don King for a Lewis–Holyfield fight, tentatively scheduled for Las Vegas on 25 April 1998. But Lewis was sceptical, admitting: 'I will believe it when I see Holyfield in the opposite corner.'

The doubts proved well founded when Holyfield made excessive financial demands and even though Lewis said he would be willing to take a $5m pay cut to make the fight, a deal could not be agreed.

With the collapse of the Holyfield bout, Lewis was forced to look elsewhere for his next opponent. One was found in the shape of Shannon Briggs, who Lewis would face in a voluntary defence before a proposed mandatory against the Croatian Zeljko Mavrovic. Although Briggs was a big, fit and ambitious fighter with fast hands, he had yet to push himself into the higher echelons of the heavyweight division. He wasn't expected to cause Lewis too many problems.

Briggs, 26, had been raised in the same Brownsville district of Brooklyn, New York that spawned fellow heavyweights Riddick Bowe and Mike Tyson. After a solid amateur career, Briggs missed out on the 1992 Barcelona Olympics when he was forced to withdraw from the trials with an injured hand. Briggs then turned professional and won his first 25 fights, including 15 in the first round. Likeable, exciting and articulate, Briggs was tipped to go all the way to the top, but at least some of those predictions changed after his next fight in Atlantic City on 15 March 1996. He was matched with a trial-horse named Darroll Wilson, who was expected to fold in much the same manner as Briggs's previous opponents. Instead, Wilson survived an early shellacking to leave Briggs a bloodied mess on the canvas in the third round. The referee did not even bother to count.

The devastating manner of the defeat cast serious doubt on Briggs's future. He blamed his collapse on asthma brought on by dust mites in his hotel room and vowed to continue his career. Within 20 months, Briggs got the chance to put himself back in the heavyweight shake-up when he was matched with the veteran two-time world champion George Foreman in Atlantic City on 22 November 1997.

Briggs beat Foreman via a controversial majority decision, with almost everyone in the arena bar the judges believing Foreman had won comfortably. The debateable victory earned Briggs a shot at Lewis's WBC title.

At 26, Briggs was six years younger than Lewis but the champion had mixed in a far higher company. That didn't stop Briggs predicting: 'This is my destiny. The belt is mine. Even if I didn't want it, it would be mine. There's nothing anyone can do about it.'

Lewis countered: 'In a room full of men, I'll always be the last man standing. This isn't going to be easy for Briggs. He has only had one important fight. But it takes years and many fights to get mentally as well as physically strong. I don't want to fight old guys. I'm giving a younger man a chance to make a name for himself. I've got to take him seriously.'

Lewis's trainer Emanuel Steward appeared to give Briggs little chance of winning when he claimed: 'Lennox has got everything: size, power and boxing skills. If it wasn't for boxing politics he would already be known as the best ever.'

In the days leading up to the fight, rumours circulated that Briggs had injured his hand in training and was undergoing treatment. But with two days to go, Maloney said: 'There is nothing wrong with Briggs's hand. It is just a rumour spread by a rival promoter to sabotage the show. I have no doubt Briggs will fight and will be one hundred per cent fit.'

The bout went ahead and turned out to be one of the most exciting in the heavyweight division for years. Lewis was staggered and almost overwhelmed in the first round but recovered to overpower a game Briggs, dropping him twice in the fourth and once in the fifth. Once again, Lewis's big right hand did most of the damage. The fight was stopped with an exhausted Briggs on the floor not from the effects of a punch but from the momentum of one last desperate left hook that Lewis avoided.

Afterwards, Briggs said: 'I would have preferred to have been stopped for getting hit rather than for missing with a punch. Lewis is a great champion. Strong and fast. I came close to being the heavyweight champion of the world. It was a great experience. I could have been in control more, but Lewis is a real champion. He proved himself and came back.'

Timothy Smith of the *New York Times* took a different view, branding Lewis's performance 'lethargic'. 'Whether Lewis was impressive enough to lure Holyfield into a bout is questionable,' Smith wrote. 'On the other hand, the way Lewis struggled against Briggs, Holyfield may be more confident than ever that he can defeat Lewis and claim all three belts.'

The fight was coming and Lewis needed it. After the Briggs bout, it was clear that if he was ever going to get the recognition he felt he deserved in the US, he would have to meet and beat Holyfield.

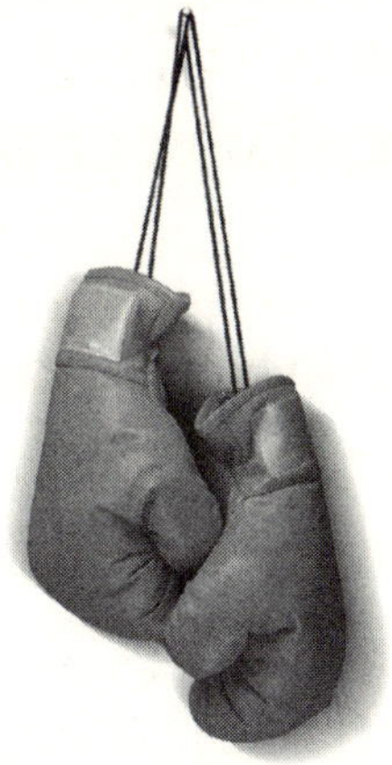

Fight 35

ZELJKO MAVROVIC

WBC heavyweight title

Venue: Mohegan Sun Casino, Uncasville, Connecticut, USA

Date: 26 September 1998

Scheduled distance: Twelve rounds

Weights: Lewis 243lbs; Mavrovic 214½lbs

Records: Lewis 33-1; Mavrovic 27-0

Result: Lewis won pts 12

MORE than ever, Lennox Lewis was now hankering after a career-defining unification bout with WBA and IBF champion Evander Holyfield, but his short-term hopes were soon dashed. It was announced that Holyfield would next be meeting Lewis's old rival and WBA number one contender Henry Akinwande on 6 June 1998. With Holyfield's immediate future tied up, it was proposed that Lewis would next meet the WBC number one contender Zeljko Mavrovic in the Croatian capital city of Zagreb. Purse bids for the bout were put on hold by the WBC to enable the Lewis camp to negotiate a seven-fight deal with HBO. At the end of June, a deal between the two parties was struck and a no-strings $20m offer was made to Holyfield to meet Lewis on 5 or 12 December. Lewis would first go through with the Mavrovic bout and Holyfield would meet Akinwande in late August. However, the Akinwande fight was cancelled when the challenger contracted hepatitis B.

Instead, Holyfield agreed to face his IBF mandatory challenger Vaughn Bean in Atlanta,

Georgia on 19 September, while Lewis would face Mavrovic the following week. If both came through, a unification match would then be held to find a true world heavyweight champion. When Holyfield beat Bean, albeit on a rather unconvincing 12-round points decision, it became imperative that Lewis did not slip up against Mavrovic.

Although Mavrovic was unbeaten in 27 fights, with 22 wins inside the distance, he was not well known in America. The vast majority of his bouts had been in Germany against mediocre European journeymen. Even though the bout ended up taking place in the US, interest was minimal. Mavrovic was considered a solid performer with a good chin, but if powerful punchers like Tommy Morrison and Andrew Golota couldn't budge Lewis, what chance did Mavrovic have? He had never met anyone of Lewis's size and power before.

To prepare for the bout, Mavrovic abandoned the modern facilities he usually used in Chicago and travelled to his native Croatia. His trainer John 'Darkie' Smith said: 'In Croatia it's very rugged, which Zeljko prefers. While

Lewis will be in camp for two months, Zeljko's been getting ready for eight. We've been doing a range of things at different stages to bring him to where we want him. He's already done plenty of good, fast sparring for conditioning.'

Smith was also confident his man could pull off an upset. 'Yes, he [Lewis] is very, very powerful but he has three or four flaws we intend taking advantage of,' Smith said. 'Lewis hasn't the greatest chin. Oliver McCall done him and so would Shannon Briggs if he'd known how to finish. Nowadays it seems when Lennox gets hit on the chops, he doesn't know whether he wants to be a fighter or lying on some beach in the Caribbean. I think Lennox will come out trying to finish us early because he'll think he has the power and the bulk. But he may come unstuck because Zeljko isn't Andrew Golota. He won't stand like a rabbit in the car's headlights. You can only go with the tools you've got and whatever Emanuel Steward says about Lennox I know my fighter is every bit as good.'

Steward played down Mavrovic's credentials, retorting: 'It's really a no-win situation even with Lennox winning with an early knockout. People in the States don't know Mavrovic even though he has a 27-0 record with 22 knockouts, but there's not a name on that record anybody would recognise. It's one of the least impressive records I've ever seen in my life, but Mavrovic winds up as the WBC's number one contender. How does that happen?'

Lewis agreed, adding: 'Mavrovic was a good amateur and he is surprisingly undefeated despite not having a knockout punch. This guy has never been hit but I'm going to hit him – and hard.'

Mavrovic, who had been out of the ring for 11 months, sported a Mohawk haircut, a nod to his admiration of the Mohawk Indians. The bout, easily the biggest of Mavrovic's career, was held in a $1.5m pavilion erected in the casino's car park.

Mavrovic didn't shrink from the task. He held his ground and put up a competitive fight but lacked the firepower to turn the bout his way. Lewis tired early, later claiming he had 'trained wrong', but landed more clean punches over the 12 rounds to win by scores of 119-109, 117-112 and 117-111.

Afterwards, Lewis said: 'Look, some fighters give you hard times. He is ranked number one. I thought I would knock him out, but give him respect. He has a great chin.'

Steward admitted: 'Lennox was puffing at the end of round three. He trained properly for the fight. I just couldn't understand why he got tired.'

Mavrovic said: 'I gave my best. Lennox was the better man this night. I was so proud to be here. His uppercut was his best weapon, particularly after he recognised he could stop me with that punch.'

It was first time in more than two years that Lewis had gone the distance and once again he had shown questionable stamina. It was a perceived weakness that might have encouraged Evander Holyfield, whose shadow now loomed in Lewis's midst. Their showdown was just around the corner.

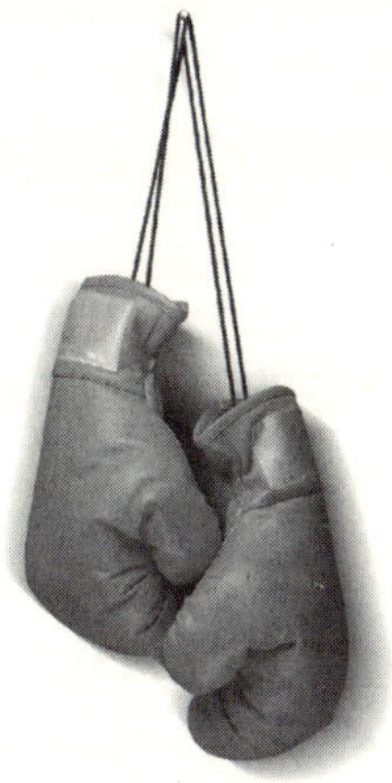

Fight 36

EVANDER HOLYFIELD I

WBC/WBA/IBF heavyweight titles

Venue: Madison Square Garden, New York, USA

Date: 13 March 1999

Scheduled distance: Twelve rounds

Weights: Lewis 245lbs; Holyfield 215lbs

Records: Lewis 34-1; Holyfield 36-3

Result: Draw

APART from their differing physical dimensions, Lennox and Evander Holyfield were cut from similar cloth. Both were dour, uncharismatic characters who preferred to do their talking in the ring and while they were occasionally caught up in controversy, neither courted it. Their showdown for all three major world heavyweight titles had been long awaited and now it was finally happening. No one, though, could have forecast what was about to unfold at Madison Square Garden, New York's so-called mecca of boxing.

In Holyfield, Lewis was meeting a naturally smaller man but one who had already commanded a reputation as one of the most fearsome competitors in the history of the sport. Holyfield also thrived on challenges. After decimating the cruiserweight division in a little over three years, many said he was too small to repeat his success as a heavyweight. They were wrong. Using a scientific training regime Holyfield added size and strength, and in just over two years won the undisputed title by knocking out James 'Buster' Douglas. But his defining win came in November 1996, when he upset the heavily favoured Mike Tyson to recapture the WBA title and become a three-time heavyweight champion.

Holyfield had also fought a classic trilogy of fights with Lewis's arch-rival Riddick Bowe. He won the second bout on points on the infamous night of the Fan Man, who landed in the ring in a motorised parachute in the middle of the seventh round. Holyfield seemed almost unmoved by the bizarre interruption and his reaction that night typified his unflappable nature.

The fight with Lewis was screened live on HBO in America and on Sky Sports in Britain. It was for all the marbles, with Lewis defending his WBC title and Holyfield risking his WBA and IBF championships. As the holder of two titles Holyfield earned $20m – double Lewis's purse – and started as a slight favourite with the oddsmakers.

Holyfield, at 36 the older man by three years, praised Lewis before the bout, confessing: 'He's strong, has a good jab, decent skills, but you can't tell how good a fighter he really is until he fights someone good and uses everything he knows. He showed some of that against [Ray] Mercer. In that fight, Lennox showed me things I never thought he had.'

Uncharacteristically, Holyfield put pressure on himself by predicting he would knock Lewis out in the third round. Lou Duva, Holyfield's former trainer, said in a report published in the *New York Times*: 'I know Evander. If he gave you a promise, he's going to try to fulfil it. He's going to try to knock him out in the third round. That will open him up to Lewis's right hand.'

Lewis made light of the prediction, scoffing: 'I can't understand why he said he'd win in three. He's never beaten anyone [of note] that quick. This fight will leave my name in stone.'

Lewis outweighed Holyfield by 31 pounds in the battle of champions but the American said his opponent was simply a 'big target'. Holyfield told the final news conference three days before the fight: 'When a person is a target is when a person can get hit. What to do? Hit him.'

Holyfield did that but not nearly enough to win the fight, or even come close. After 12 rounds, the bout was declared a draw, which to most was an outrageously inaccurate reflection of what happened in the ring. The result was booed by the crowd of 21,284, the large majority of whom had Lewis dominating the fight. Punch statistics showed Lewis landing nearly three times as many blows – 348 to 130. In six of the 12 rounds, Holyfield was credited with landing fewer than ten punches.

HBO's Jim Lampley told viewers: 'That is, ladies and gentlemen, a travesty, an outrage, a highway robbery. Lennox Lewis has just been robbed. He won it and he didn't get it.'

Lewis, who looked perplexed when the decision was announced, said afterwards: 'I am the undisputed heavyweight champion of the world. What you saw in there was called politics. It was my time to shine and they ripped me off. What do I see now? Automatic rematch next month. I doubt he wants to box me again.' Lewis's trainer Emanuel Steward said: 'It wasn't even close. This is what is killing boxing.'

While South African judge Stanley Christodoulou had Lewis winning, posting a score of 116-113, the two who didn't – American Eugenia Williams, who scored 115-113 for Holyfield, and Britain's Larry O'Connell, who had the fight even at 115-115 – both defended their version of events, claiming they scored the bout as they saw it.

But the decision attracted widespread condemnation. Timothy Smith of the *New York Daily News* said it was akin to a 'Brink truck heist'. The legendary Muhammad Ali went even further, describing the result as the 'biggest fix in fight history'. In a letter to senator John McCain, published in the *New York Post*, Ali wrote: 'As the former three-time heavyweight champion of the world, I believe I have the credibility to say Lennox Lewis won this bout without question and should have been named the clear victor. What occurred once the 12-round event concluded will surely go down in the boxing annals as the biggest fix in fight history. The rush of emotions that ran through me the moment the decision was declared ranged from total disbelief to outrage.'

The only possible solution to the controversy was a rematch but it couldn't happen immediately. The dust had to settle before they could do it again, and next time Lewis had to make sure he left nothing to chance.

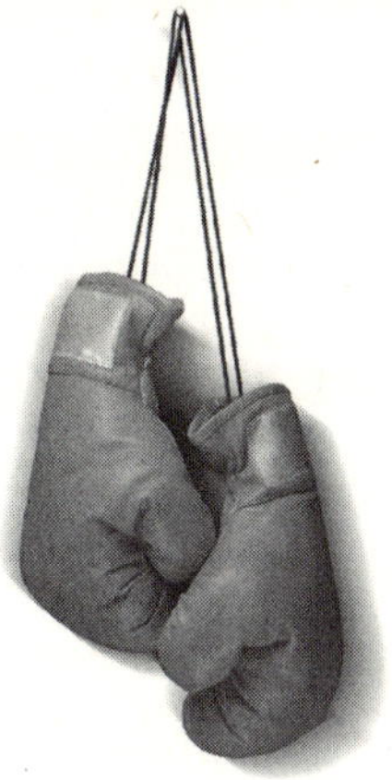

Fight 37

EVANDER HOLYFIELD II

WBC/WBA/IBF heavyweight titles

Venue: Thomas & Mack Center, Las Vegas, USA

Date: 13 November 1999

Scheduled distance: Twelve rounds

Weights: Lewis 242lbs; Holyfield 217lbs

Records: Lewis 34-1-1; Holyfield 36-3-1

Result: Lewis won pts 12

THE bitter aftermath of the first fight between Lennox Lewis and Evander Holyfield had left a sour taste and lent added significance to the rematch eight months later. Boxing could not afford another black eye that would give its critics yet more ammunition. After a bad year all round, the fight needed to pass without controversy and preferably produce a clear, conclusive winner, whichever way it went. Public sympathy was with Lewis, so he went into the return bout as both the betting and sentimental favourite.

In an article in *The Independent* the day before the fight, it was suggested that both boxers shared a collective responsibility to help restore the sport's battered image. 'As the hour draws near, Holyfield–Lewis II has come to seem less of a mere title decider than boxing's last best hope for redemption,' it read.

The fighters split $30m, reflecting the perceived injustice of the first fight, for which Holyfield had earned considerably more. 'If it means taking less then I will take less,' Holyfield said. 'If I fought a great fight, I wouldn't be sliding down.'

Lewis's determination was clearly evident in the build-up. 'I showed Evander too much respect last time,' he said. 'I'm going to step up the pace and utilise my talent. I'm going to come out strong and keep it going. You're only as good as your last fight, but I hope I can wipe that bad taste out of my mouth. Those thinking Holyfield's going to win are living in a dream world. If Evander fights any better, it will bring out the best in me. The only thing he's going to be is older. The world is starving for a good fight and I'm going to do my part and everything possible to make it so.'

Holyfield, who was not normally given to offering excuses, said he had been affected by stomach cramps from the third round of the first fight, telling the media: 'I had to fight when I didn't really want to. I wasn't willing to give up because I wasn't feeling good. I don't take anything away from Lennox. He fought a great fight. My opinion of him went up. But I'm happy he didn't get the best of me. I've played the tape of the fight over and over and I've always been able to correct mistakes. I can't put myself in a position of being a loser. The difference in this fight is that I know what he's capable of doing.'

He didn't know enough. After an absorbing but far from compelling fight that was much closer, Lewis was awarded a unanimous points decision, winning by scores of 116-112, 117-111 and 115-113. For Lewis, it represented justice after the drawn verdict in the first fight, which he had dominated. But although there was no controversy this time, certain sections of the American press tried to concoct one by claiming that Holyfield, who was far more aggressive, should have got the decision.

Wallace Matthews of the *New York Post* claimed the judges 'should be subjected to even more scrutiny than those two hapless souls faced after the Agony at the Garden'.

Matthews wrote: 'With the exception of the way he fought the ninth round, Lennox Lewis had little to be proud of last night. In a fight that had two great rounds, two good ones and nearly a half-hour of posing, pawing and clinching, the names you will remember today are [judges] Bill Graham, Jerry Roth and Chuck Giampa. They are the ones who decided that last night would be Lennox Lewis's night, even after Holyfield had cut him, shook him up in the third, nearly stopped him in the seventh and pushed him all over the ring in the 12th.'

Despite Matthews' assertions, this time the decision was supported by the post-fight numbers. Lewis threw and landed more punches than Holyfield, although the margin of difference was much smaller than in the first bout.

Lewis, who had been roared on by 6,000 Brits, told the Associated Press: 'I couldn't let my fans down. I couldn't let myself down because this was my dream.' Holyfield said: 'Decisions are decisions. Everyone is disappointed, but life is life. I was just fighting. The judges make the decisions.'

The decision was that after a long, arduous journey Lewis was now the undisputed heavyweight champion of the world. There was still a little way to go, and there would be one more bump in the road, but in the months ahead Lewis would be out to show the rest of the division exactly who was boss.

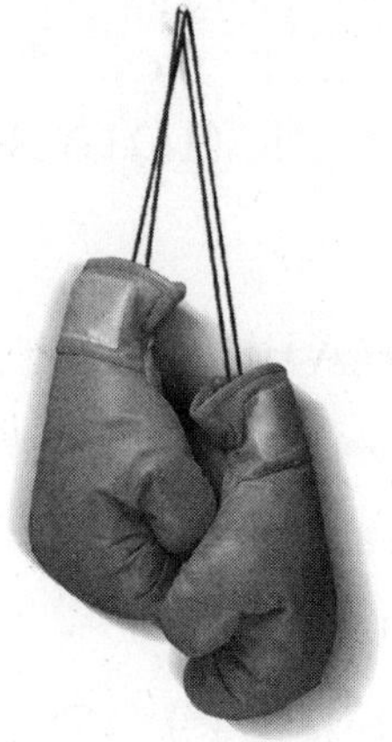

Fight 38

MICHAEL GRANT

WBC/IBF heavyweight titles

Venue: Madison Square Garden, New York, USA

Date: 29 April 2000

Scheduled distance: Twelve rounds

Weights: Lewis 247lbs; Grant 250lbs

Records: Lewis 35-1-1; Grant 31-0

Result: Lewis won KO2

MICHAEL GRANT

MICHAEL Grant was poster-boy material. Tall, dark and handsome, with a torso that looked like it had been carved out of stone, the unbeaten 27-year-old was the best of the prospects coming through in America. Although still comparatively raw, Grant had survived a torrid test against Poland's Andrew Golota in his previous fight and was ready to step up to the next level. That meant challenging Lewis in the Briton's first defence since becoming undisputed world heavyweight champion five months earlier.

Almost inevitably, there were political complications. In agreeing to face Grant, Lewis had breached a contract stipulating that he would meet the WBA number one contender if he won his rematch with Evander Holyfield. At the time, that was Henry Akinwande, a fighter Lewis had already beaten. When Akinwande was ruled unfit to fight on medical grounds, he was replaced by the Puerto Rican John Ruiz, who had beaten no-one of note and was considered undeserving of the mandatory position. Ruiz had also been knocked out in 19 seconds by the big-punching New Zealander

David Tua, now the IBF mandatory challenger, who had pressed his own claims in court in an effort to force Lewis to face him next.

Despite Ruiz's spurious elevation, Lewis was stripped of the WBA title he had taken from Holyfield and instead met Grant, a former college sports standout, with only the WBC and IBF championships at stake. In reality, it made no difference to Lewis's standing as he was now universally considered the true – and lineal – heavyweight champion. Before the fight, Lewis told *newson6.com*: 'I'm just going out to show I'm the best fighter on the planet.'

Grant, 27, was unbeaten in 31 bouts, winning 22 inside the distance. The previous November, he had stepped up to face Golota, who was only two years removed from his quickfire defeat by Lewis. Down and almost out in the first round, Grant fought back with his eyes swelling to drop Golota in the tenth, when the Pole indicated he did not want to carry on.

Although huge at 6ft 7in and heavily muscled, Grant was fast and mobile. He also had power, particularly in the right hand. A polite, clean-living churchgoer, Grant was a friend and stablemate of Holyfield's and took a giant leap of faith in predicting he would win.

'Evander will have to live with me having his titles,' Grant told Jeff Powell of *The Mail*. 'He understands better than anyone when I say that I've had a vision of how I'm going to knock out Lennox. Lennox is gutsy but not as gutsy as me. I proved that to myself when I got up from being caught by Andrew Golota and stopped him.'

Grant said coming through the Golota fight had lifted him to a new level mentally. 'I have no fear of being hit now, not even by the biggest punchers, because I know I can take it,' Grant said. 'On top of that, I'm not only bigger than Lennox but I'm more athletic, more mobile and faster. I've also got a lot more stamina. I've noticed that he gets lackadaisical later in his fights and stops punching. I've been dreaming of this fight for the last few years. I am the future of world heavyweight boxing.'

He wasn't. After a fast start, Grant ended up hopelessly out of his depth. Lewis hammered him with right hands, putting him down three times in the first round. Only Grant's fighting heart got him out of it. Although he hung in for most of the second as Lewis hunted him down, Grant couldn't escape. With the round ticking down, a right uppercut caught the challenger flush as he was bending low and sent him to the canvas again, where he was counted out.

'I was very surprised when he came at me,' Lewis said in a report by Bill Pennington of the *New York Daily News*. 'I realised it was only a matter of time because I realised I had superior hand speed. I could see when he was winding up, and I beat him to the punch. I held my position so I could get a good shot. Every time I hit him he went down, so I just kept hitting him.'

Grant said: 'I just got caught, that's all. Lennox is a champion for a reason. He'd fought the best out there. He caught me and it pretty much stunned me for the rest of the knockdowns. I wanted to come out for the second, because the intensity and determination stayed in me. But the fight was still a great experience for me.'

As in his fights against Razor Ruddock and Andrew Golota, Lewis had shown just how devastating he could be when fully motivated against the right opponent. But as far as the

American press were concerned, he didn't do it enough. To consider him great – and Lewis's trainer Emanuel Steward believed he had the tools to be better than Muhammad Ali – they wanted him to show passion and aggression every time he fought instead of falling back on his safety-first approach. Yes, Lewis had his weaknesses and many sceptics in America had still to fully warm to him. But they had to accept one thing: Lewis was now undeniably the best heavyweight in the world.

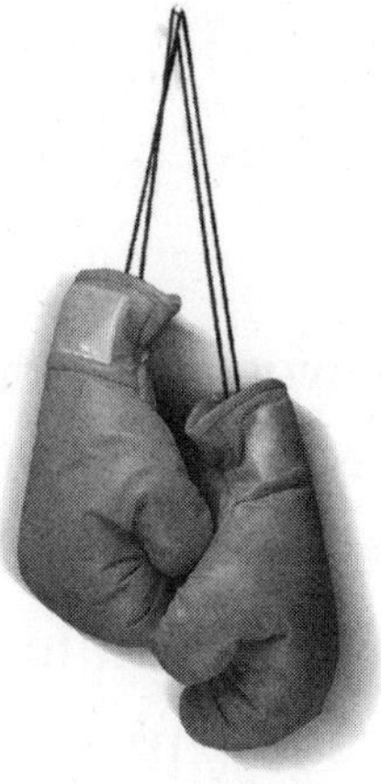

Fight 39

FRANS BOTHA

WBC/IBF heavyweight titles

Venue: London Arena, London, England

Date: 15 July 2000

Scheduled distance: Twelve rounds

Weights: Lewis 250lbs; Botha 237lbs

Records: Lewis 36-1-1; Botha 40-2-1

Result: Lewis won TKO2

FRANS BOTHA

LENNOX Lewis had always intended to fight three times in 2000 and after his explosive win over Michael Grant he made a quick return to the ring with a voluntary defence against Frans Botha, the US-based South African. Having not boxed in Britain since his defeat by Oliver McCall six years earlier, it was now time for the world's top heavyweight to give his loyal British fans a glimpse of their champion in the flesh.

Lewis justifiably felt he was entitled to a defence against a less threatening opponent after his previous three bouts against Evander Holyfield, a three-time world champion, and Grant, the best of the young contenders. Botha fitted the bill. He was strong and tough, had a good record and a decent chin. Botha was also a former IBF champion, although he did not quite have the tools to mix it at the highest level.

Nevertheless, he cleverly combined the attributes he did possess, namely his striking appearance and the fact he was a white heavyweight in a black-dominated division, to land some high-profile fights.

In January 1999, Botha put up stubborn resistance against a rusty Mike Tyson, who was returning from an 18-month suspension for biting Holyfield's ears in a title fight. In a dirty, bad-tempered bout in Las Vegas, Botha foiled and frustrated Tyson before walking on to a fight-ending right hand in the fifth round. The South African had also been stopped in 11 rounds by Michael Moorer in an abortive attempt to regain the IBF title in 1996. He had won it a year earlier against the German Axel Schulz before being stripped over a positive steroid test.

Botha, 31, was considered to have little chance of upsetting Lewis, who was treating the fight as a homecoming. 'There will be no McCall repeat,' Lewis said in a report published in *The Telegraph* before the fight. 'I won't get caught again. My immediate challenge is to dispose of Botha as quickly as possible. People like Frans Botha are fighting an uphill battle because I have full confidence every time I go into the ring.'

Trainer Emanuel Steward, in a moment of hyperbole that wouldn't have disgraced Don

King, described Lewis as 'the best heavyweight in the history of boxing'. George Kimball, writing in the *Irish Times*, observed: 'The Las Vegas sports books make Lewis a 13-1 on favourite, and the odds should probably be longer than that.

'Botha's slim chances rest on two far-fetched hopes: the possibility that Lewis may have been distracted by all the Tyson talk which has dominated the run-up to Saturday night's homecoming, and the memory of Lewis's last London fight six years ago, when Oliver McCall caught the heavyweight champion napping at Wembley and knocked him silly.'

But Sterling McPherson, Botha's American trainer, warned everyone to prepare for a surprise. 'I'm serious,' he told the *Las Vegas Sun*. 'Lewis and his people think they're getting some fat, roly-poly guy and that they're going to have a walk in the park. But this is Botha we're talking about and I think he has a very solid chance of pulling this off.

'You have to have the mental capacity to handle fights of this magnitude and Botha has proven he can do it. He's no Johnny-come-lately.

'If Lewis is depending on his conditioning from the Grant fight and hasn't been working hard – which I heard he wasn't – then he's in for a rude awakening.

'Grant was scared to death and that fearfulness cost him the fight. But Botha's not afraid of anyone and he's not going to run out there like Grant did and get himself knocked out.'

That's what McPherson thought. When Lewis and Botha stood opposite each other in the ring, they looked like fighters from different weight divisions. They might as well have been. The writing was on the wall as early as the first round, when Botha staggered backwards after taking a right hand. At the end of the second, Lewis landed a stunning three-punch combination and the fight was over. Botha ended up face-first through the ropes. He rose but looked unsteady and the fight was stopped.

For the second fight in a row, Lewis had well and truly hit the power button. Afterwards, he addressed the persistent speculation over a future fight with Tyson, who had recently fought twice in Britain. 'Tell Mike Tyson to put up or shut up,' Lewis told the Associated Press in a report published on *cbsnews.com*. 'He keeps talking about what he can eat. I'll show him what he can eat.' Lewis was referring to his right hand in response to Tyson's crass claim after his controversial win over Lou Savarese in Glasgow the previous month that he 'wanted to eat his [Lewis's] children'.

Next, though, Lewis would have to negotiate a threat that was arguably even more perilous than that presented by Tyson. Looming on the horizon was a mandatory defence against the power-punching Kiwi David Tua.

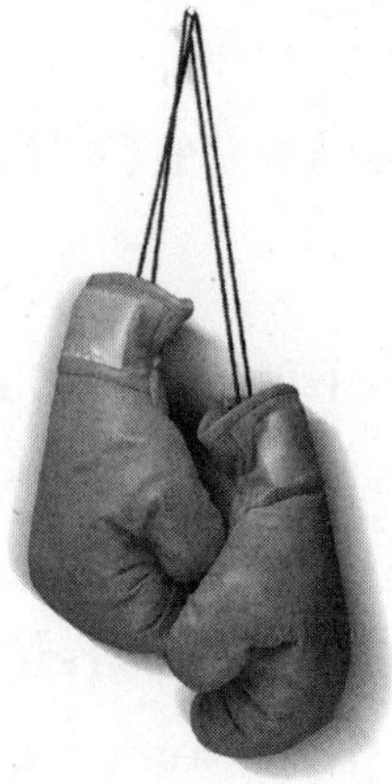

Fight 40

DAVID TUA

WBC/IBF heavyweight titles

Venue: Mandalay Bay Events Center, Las Vegas, USA

Date: 11 November 2000

Scheduled distance: Twelve rounds

Weights: Lewis 249lbs; Tua 245lbs

Records: Lewis 37-1-1; Tua 37-1

Result: Lewis won pts 12

DAVID TUA was an out-and-out destroyer. With a series of spine-tingling knockouts on cable TV in America, the Samoan-born New Zealander had catapulted himself into heavyweight title contention. Built along similar lines to Mike Tyson and Joe Frazier, Tua went into the ring with one thing on his mind: to obliterate his opponent. He now intended to do the same to Lennox Lewis.

Their fight, a mandatory IBF title defence for Lewis, was eagerly awaited. The squat, bull-like Tua, 27, was stepping up for the biggest test of his career, while Lewis was risking his reputation against the most chilling puncher in the division. The *Washington Post* ran a pre-fight story under the headline 'David vs Goliath'. In Tua's adopted homeland, 85,000 bets were placed on the fight, the *New Zealand Herald* reported. The TAB betting agency took $2.6m in total, most of which was wagered on the local favourite.

Tua, a bronze medallist at the 1992 Olympics in Barcelona, had shot to notice with a murderous 19-second KO of future champion

John Ruiz in Atlantic City in March 1996. The following year, Tua suffered his first defeat but lost nothing when outpointed by the talented Nigerian Ike Ibeabuchi, who subsequently lost his way outside the ring and failed to fulfil his potential. Together, he and Tua threw more than 1,100 punches in 12 rounds, a record for a heavyweight fight.

Now came Lewis. 'I'm confident I'll win,' the much shorter Tua predicted before the fight. 'Lennox is a big fighter, but I'm better. I'm ready to go toe-to-toe with him.' It was Tua's only chance of victory but Lewis was never going to give it to him. 'Tua's not going to be the man to make a name off beating me,' Lewis said. 'He has been fighting guys who can't take a punch. I'm concerned about his power, but that's his only asset. Unless I stick out my chin and allow him to hit it, he doesn't have a chance to take me out. I won't make it possible.'

Most experts saw the bout as a dress rehearsal for Lewis's proposed fight with Tyson, even though the former champion was now threatening to call time on his career. 'Once Lewis dispatches Tua, Tyson won't see much incentive to overturn his retirement,' wrote Tim Graham of *espn.com*.

Lewis's trainer Emanuel Steward saw it clearly. 'Lennox Lewis is too much for Tua,' he said. 'Lennox has a great right uppercut and a great overhand right. This is a fight between a good big man and good little man. The size will be the difference.'

Steward was right. Boxing smartly, Lewis kept Tua at bay with his jab, which accounted for more than two-thirds of his total punches, and generally nullified him to score a one-sided unanimous points decision. The scores were 119-109, 118-110 and 117-111. Tua, who had scored 32 knockouts against lower-level opponents, rarely got close enough to test Lewis's chin.

Afterwards, the Tua camp revealed their man had aggravated a rib injury sustained in sparring two months earlier. But Lewis, quoted in a report by Ed Schuyler in *The Independent*, quipped: 'I had a knee injury, a nose injury and an ear injury. I was wondering if he was aware of those. What was wrong with David Tua was Lennox Lewis. He had never seen a Lennox Lewis. You can say what you want, but you have to bring it to the ring. I was doing all the work in the fight. If you come to war, you have to bring your whole arsenal, not just a left hook and a haircut.'

The topic of discussion inevitably returned to Tyson, a fight with whom was the only thing Lewis needed to cement his legacy. 'He deserves it,' Lewis's manager Frank Maloney told BBC Radio Five Live. 'He was robbed of a fight against Riddick Bowe. He was robbed of a fight with Michael Moorer when Moorer was in his prime. Tyson's been out there and has always been like a shadow. He's made a lot of noises about how great he is, and how he wants the belt. Well, Lennox Lewis has got the belt. If he wants it, come and get it.'

Tyson wouldn't be coming for it just yet, but someone else would be. His name was Hasim Rahman – and Lewis would never forget him.

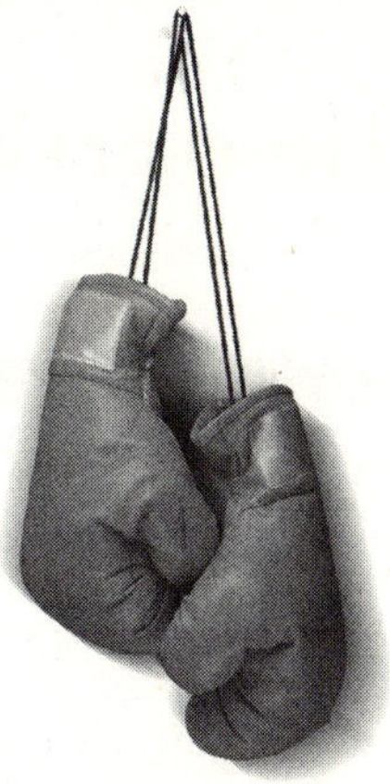

Fight 41

HASIM RAHMAN I

WBC/IBF heavyweight titles

Venue: Carnival City, Johannesburg, South Africa

Date: 22 April 2001

Scheduled distance: Twelve rounds

Weights: Lewis 253½lbs; Rahman 238lbs

Records: Lewis 38-1-1; Rahman 34-2

Result: Lewis lost KO5

LENNOX Lewis and Hasim Rahman were on different planes, the proverbial breed apart. Lewis was flying high, enjoying new-found respect, if not universal affection, as the undisputed world heavyweight champion. By contrast, Rahman was just another opponent, a one-time prospect who could punch but had lost his two biggest fights against David Tua and Oleg Maskaev. The result looked such a foregone conclusion that the fight was virtually ignored by American writers.

Perhaps they should have known better. A cursory glance at the history books would have told them the pieces were already in place for a major upset. A heavily favoured and apparently complacent champion was thousands of miles from home and about to go in with a huge outsider no one was giving a prayer. It was the same story before Mike Tyson was knocked out by James 'Buster' Douglas in Tokyo, Japan in 1990 and before George Foreman was humbled by Muhammad Ali in Kinshasa, Zaire 16 years earlier. On the wrong day, against the wrong opponent, absolutely anything could happen.

It did.

Lewis, blithely unconcerned by the threat Rahman posed, arrived in high-altitude Johannesburg less than two weeks before the fight, delayed by his involvement in the movie *Ocean's Eleven*. It was being filmed in Las Vegas, where Lewis had been training. By contrast Rahman, a 20-1 underdog, had already been in South Africa for a month and was fully acclimatised to the unforgiving conditions.

'Lewis has fought everybody, but I'm the strongest heavyweight in the world,' Rahman boasted before the fight. 'Sometimes he seems unbeatable, sometimes he seems ordinary, sometimes he even looks like he shouldn't be champ. When I knock Lewis out, I don't want to hear about a lucky punch, or lucky anything.'

Rahman's words echoed the bluster of Oliver McCall, another rank outsider, who had ended Lewis's first reign in a stunning upset in London seven years earlier. No one, though, seriously thought there would be a repeat.

They were wrong. Cut on the left eyelid and behind on all three scorecards after four rounds, Rahman swung for glory in the fifth. With a tiring Lewis backed up on the ropes and grinning, Rahman saw his chance. He stepped in and poleaxed Lewis with a picture-perfect right hand that felled the champion like a tree. It was McCall all over again. Lewis's titles had gone.

Afterwards, Rahman told the Associated Press: 'I kept my prayers going and did all my training. And I came up with one punch. *One* punch.'

The result sent shockwaves through boxing and sparked celebration in Rahman's home city. John Murphy of the *Baltimore Sun* reported: 'Viewed as a low-risk assignment by Lewis, Rahman beat the odds and brought the heavyweight title back to the United States and, for the first time ever, to the city of Baltimore.'

The real truth, though, was that Lewis had beaten himself. At a press conference in Las Vegas two weeks earlier, he was heard to casually dismiss not only the challenger but the physical limitations of fighting at altitude, where reduced oxygen levels make it harder to breathe.

'I could hardly believe what I was hearing,' Glenn McCrory, a former Lewis opponent and

Sky TV commentator, told John Rawling in an interview for *The Guardian* eight months later. 'There was Lennox saying that going to fight in Johannesburg, which is 6,000ft above sea level, would be no problem. He was saying that altitude would have no effect on him and that we shouldn't believe what the scientists say. It was as if he really believed that he was different from every other man.

'He thought Rahman was nothing. I admit, I thought Lennox would still be able to win if he'd been the director of that film and played all the characters. But complacency can be a problem for any athlete and it certainly was for Lennox. Rahman was up for the fight and Lennox just wasn't there.'

Even after the fight, Lewis tried to play down the role most believe he had played in his own downfall. 'I felt fine in there,' he insisted. 'I was going about my work nice and comfortably and there was no way Hasim Rahman could beat me. This is just what happens in heavyweight boxing. He hit me with a good shot. That's the situation when you get two big guys in there with right hands.'

Lewis's trainer Emanuel Steward said: 'Lennox just got hit on the chin. That is what makes this sport so dramatic. It is just one loss.'

Bob Mee, covering for *The Telegraph*, cut through the artifice when he wrote: 'After the fight Lewis seemed in complete denial, and his team closed ranks to support him. Loyalty has its place, but in private there should be some hard talking.'

The defeat threatened to scupper Lewis's mooted megafight with Mike Tyson, who was now in Rahman's sights. If Lewis was going to restore credibility and eventually land a fight with Tyson, he would first have to come back and regain his titles. In the past, Lewis had always been a different animal when he had something to prove. Now the beast would have to return again.

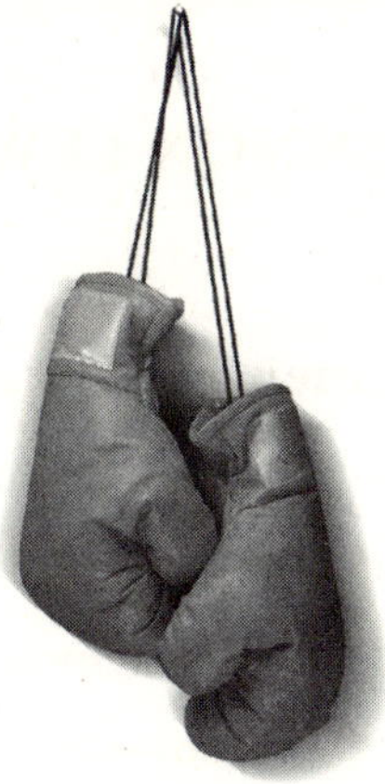

Fight 42

HASIM RAHMAN II

WBC/IBF heavyweight titles

Venue: Mandalay Bay, Las Vegas, USA

Date: 17 November 2001

Scheduled distance: Twelve rounds

Weights: Lewis 246½lbs; Rahman 236lbs

Records: Lewis 38-2-1; Rahman 35-2

Result: Lewis won KO4

LENNOX Lewis's back was against the wall and it usually spelt danger for his opponents. He had been in the same position before and it had driven him to deliver some of his most destructive performances to date. This time, though, there was no margin for error. In order to secure the career-defining fight he wanted against Mike Tyson, Lewis had to beat Hasim Rahman in their rematch and do it conclusively.

Despite the nature of his defeat in Johannesburg, most observers appeared to be of the opinion that Lewis had beaten himself. This view was shared by the oddsmakers, who installed Lewis as a 7-2 on favourite to regain his titles. He was also earning $11m, more than double Rahman's guarantee.

Lewis, who had parted company with long-time manager Frank Maloney less than two weeks before the fight, said the prospect of revenge over Rahman had 'rekindled a flame'. After the weigh-in, Lewis said: 'Rahman thinks he is king of the world, thinks he has won the lottery. Well, I'm just about to take away the ticket. Don't miss this. It's the big one. I may not be saying as much as him, but I feel thunder. Enough has been said, it's time for action. Time for me to close that mouth of his. The guy is a one-punch wonder.'

Lewis's trainer Emanuel Steward sounded less than certain about the outcome. 'No one knows what Lennox Lewis is going to do when he comes out to fight,' Steward said in a report in the Canadian newspaper the *Globe and Mail*. 'We don't know what he's going to do. He's very unpredictable. Everything is the first round of this fight. That's my biggest worry. Rahman is going to come out and take it to the street right away.'

Rahman, who had turned down several lucrative TV deals to sign with promoter Don King, was certainly not short on confidence after his stunning victory seven months earlier. 'Whatever he [Lewis] thinks, I welcome the challenge,' he told a conference call from his training camp in Big Bear, California, reported the *Las Vegas Sun*. 'I'm big in his head. I can punch hard and I'm going to mix my arsenal up. I'm psychologically, physically and mentally stronger than Lennox Lewis. I know

I humiliated this man. I knocked him out and took his titles. The facts speak for themselves.'

Interest in the bout, which was already high, had intensified when the fighters got into a scuffle on ESPN's *Up Close* TV show after Rahman had questioned Lewis's sexuality. That made the fight personal.

It came out in the ring. After dominating the first three rounds, Lewis swung a right hand at Rahman in the fourth that made him back off. He was measuring his distance. About a minute later, Lewis stepped to his left, threw a jab-cum-hook and followed it instantly with another arcing right. Rahman didn't see it. The blow zeroed in like a missile and exploded on his chin, laying him out flat, arms spreadeagled. The fight was over.

'Lennox threw one of the great combinations in the history of boxing,' Steward told Dave Anderson of the *New York Times*. 'The left was not supposed to land, just to get him [Rahman] to move into the right hand that did land.'

Lewis, accused in the past of lacking passion, celebrated as if he meant it. No wonder.

He had gained revenge and saved the fight that within months would cement his legacy. 'I said the belts were on loan,' Lewis said in a report published in the *Washington Post*. 'He [Rahman] had his 15 minutes of fame. Now the belts come home.'

Paul Hayward, reporting in *The Telegraph*, spelt out the significance of Lewis's victory. 'On a weekend when a new mega-resort called Aladdin was being saved from bankruptcy, boxing defied deflationary pressure by scrambling to arrange the most lucrative fight in heavyweight history,' wrote Hayward.

The way was now clear for the fight the world wanted: Lewis versus Tyson. All that remained was to work out the date, terms and conditions – and both sides were on it from the moment Lewis's big right hand had hit its target.

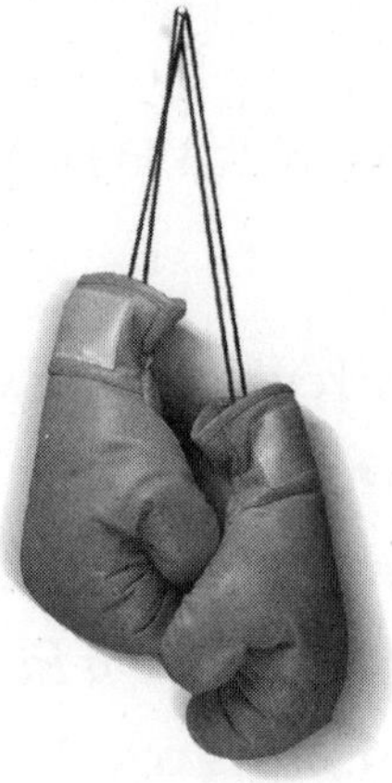

Fight 43

MIKE TYSON

WBC/IBF heavyweight titles

Venue: The Pyramid, Memphis, Tennessee, USA

Date: 8 June 2002

Scheduled distance: Twelve rounds

Weights: Lewis 249¼lbs; Tyson 234lbs

Records: Lewis 39-2-1; Tyson 49-3

Result: Lewis won KO8

MIKE TYSON was like a force of nature when he burst on to the heavyweight scene as a bull-necked 18-year-old in 1985. Mentored by Cus D'Amato, the legendary fight manager who had handled Floyd Patterson in the 1950s, Tyson had speed, ferocious power and an intimidating presence that had many opponents beaten before they even got into the ring. Like a comic-book hero, Tyson sent his early foes flying through the air as he evaded and delivered punches in the same seamless motion. The reformed street thug who loved pigeons quickly became a major draw in his native New York and it wasn't long before the rest of America, and the world, caught on.

While still only 20, Tyson won two world heavyweight titles, becoming the youngest-ever champion in the process. By 21, he had unified the championship. No fighter since Muhammad Ali had generated so much interest so quickly, but inevitably it was too much too soon. In the 15 years that followed before he finally faced Lennox Lewis, Tyson's life played out like a soap opera as he fell spectacularly from grace in and out of the ring before rising and falling again. As time ticked down on his career, Tyson remained an attraction as much for his unpredictability as for what was left of his fighting talents.

By the time he met Lewis, Tyson was 35 and more than a decade past his prime. His three defeats, against James 'Buster' Douglas and Evander Holyfield (twice), had amply illustrated that for all his offensive menace Tyson could not come through adversity to win. In the second fight with Holyfield, he had fouled flagrantly, biting Holyfield's ears and getting himself disqualified. But none of it mattered to Lewis. He didn't care which Tyson showed up, as long as he did. Because of Tyson's past standing and the mystique that still surrounded him, Lewis had to face him in order to achieve wider recognition as the best heavyweight of his generation. Although Lewis was ageing, if not fading, the general consensus was that he would still have too much for a significantly diminished Tyson.

'I don't feel Tyson deserves to be fighting for the heavyweight championship of the world, but Lewis himself chose to take this fight,' Lewis's trainer Emanuel Steward said in a report on *upi.com*. 'He is very determined not to just beat him, but to knock him out. I cannot see any way that Tyson is going to do anything against this fight machine.'

The fighters had history having sparred as amateurs in the Catskill Mountains in 1984, a few months before the Los Angeles Olympics. Bad blood had boiled over before a news conference to promote the fight five months earlier, with Tyson sparking a mass brawl during which he bit Lewis on the leg. As the bout drew nearer, Tyson continued to spit venom, *USA Today*'s Dan Rafael reported. 'My main objective is to be professional and to kill him,' Tyson said coldly from his training camp in Hawaii. 'That's really what it comes to. On June 8, flesh will not be enough. I will take Lennox's title, his soul and smear his pompous brains all over the ring when I hit him.'

Lewis was unperturbed, retorting: 'Through life there's evolution, and he's shown that he hasn't graduated.

'After a while we need to self-teach, and he's obviously not teaching himself. He sounds like a cartoon character when he says those things. To me, it's coming from an ignorant person.'

The fight was a huge event. Lewis and Tyson split $35m in purse money, with HBO and Showtime, the rival cable TV networks to which they were separately contracted, agreeing to work together for the first time to get the fight on. In the ring, the fighters were separated by a row of security men, just in case they wanted to start early.

It wouldn't have made any difference. The fight wasn't so much a contest as a one-sided beatdown. After a frenetic first round, Lewis took charge and Tyson gradually began to resemble an actor who had forgotten his lines. The only hope Tyson had was to get inside Lewis's jab and unload up close, but every time he came in Lewis nailed him with right uppercuts. At the end of the second round, Tyson's trainer Ronnie Shields implored: 'You have to be in this man's chest. Make this a very ugly fight now.'

Lewis was never going to allow it. By the seventh Tyson, cut over both eyes and bleeding from the nose, had slowed to a virtual standstill as Lewis hammered him with both hands. In commentary, HBO's Larry Merchant said: 'This is by far the worst beating Mike Tyson has ever taken.' Slumped in his corner at the end of the round, Tyson yelped in pain as his seconds tried to patch him up. They told him to go to work – but Tyson had nothing left.

In the eighth, with Tyson weak and dispirited, Lewis went for the kill. A vicious combination ending with a downward right hand caused Tyson to sink to his haunches, cowering under the onslaught. He rose bravely and was allowed to continue, but only seconds now separated him from defeat. Lewis attacked again and after avoiding one last desperate swing he primed Tyson for a final crushing right. It was short but it landed flush and folded Tyson in half. Bleeding and beaten, Tyson was counted out. The fight ended just as Lewis had wanted and imagined.

'Emanuel wanted me to take him out earlier,' Lewis said in a report in the *New York Times*. 'He was pleading with me. But I was waiting. Mike was ducking his head and I knew I'd catch him eventually. Once I did, it kept getting easier to hit him. I knew I would nail him with the big punch that would end it.'

Reflecting on the fight, Richard Hoffer wrote in *Sports Illustrated*: 'Just as you began to appreciate the honour of Lewis's accomplishment, you had to feel a pang of horror for Tyson, who no longer can afford the refuge of his so-called rage and now must reckon with what's left of his desperate destiny.'

Lewis's destiny had become a lot clearer. He was now on his way to longed-for recognition as the best heavyweight of his era, and arguably one of the best in history. But the journey was not quite over yet.

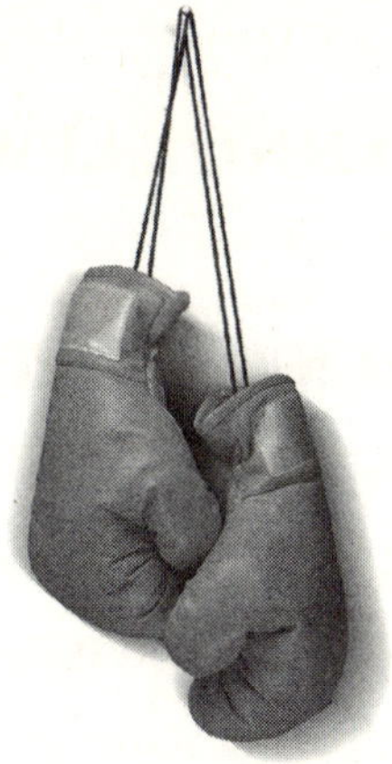

Fight 44

VITALI KLITSCHKO

WBC heavyweight title

Venue: Staples Center, Los Angeles, USA

Date: 21 June 2003

Scheduled distance: Twelve rounds

Weights: Lewis 256½lbs; Klitschko 248lbs

Records: Lewis 40-2-1; Klitschko 32-1

Result: Lewis won TKO6

VITALI Klitschko was a 21st century heavyweight, a giant who could punch his weight. The 31-year-old was the elder of the two Klitschko brothers representing Ukraine, a sovereign state in Eastern Europe. At 6ft 7in, he was one of the few fighters who could look down on Lennox Lewis, at least physically. Although not an aesthetically pleasing boxer to watch, the former WBO champion was sturdy and strong and had 31 knockouts against just one defeat, an injury retirement to Chris Byrd.

Klitschko had been due to appear on the undercard at the Staples Center after originally failing to agree a fight with Lewis, but stepped in at the 11th hour when the Canadian Kirk Johnson pulled out with a pectoral injury. Klitschko's participation ended up playing a far bigger role in Lewis's future than most expected: it persuaded the champion that his time was up.

Before the fight, Klitschko put the job of challenging Lewis into perspective. His words were a clear indication of how he intended to fight – without fear. 'We are not talking about a god here,' Klitschko said in a report in the *Irish Examiner*. 'We are all human beings. Everybody has their strengths and weaknesses. I heard Lewis say he is going to destroy me and knock me out in the first five rounds. People say I am not strong enough or in the champion's league. But I don't care what people say.'

Lewis, who had been out of the ring for a year, remained resolute in his belief that he was still number one. 'I am totally focused on this fight and there has been no complacency,' he said in a report in the *Irish Times*. 'I respect Klitschko but he is not in my class.

'Klitschko just does not have my experience or my skills and I will prove that in the ring. I am in good shape and I am ready. Now I just can't wait for the fight as he is going to get it full force.'

The fight was a war that Lewis so nearly lost. Klitschko, fighting valiantly, traded with Lewis from the start and had him rocking badly in the second and fifth rounds. But hampered by deep cuts over and under the left eye, Klitschko knew he was on borrowed time. He survived a huge right uppercut in the sixth and was starting to come on strong again as he bullied Lewis around the ring. But it was his final act of defiance. At the end of the round, the ringside doctor inspected Klitschko's injuries and stopped the fight. Once he realised what had happened, Klitschko became incandescent, shouting: 'No, no.'

Lewis had escaped. Drawn into a slugging match, he had rarely looked so wild and vulnerable. Although he said afterwards that the cuts had spared Klitschko from a knockout defeat, the truth was that it was Lewis himself who might have been saved. At the time of the stoppage, Lewis was tiring and behind 58-56 on all three scorecards, with Klitschko still well in the fight.

'Right now, I feel like the people's champion,' Klitschko said in a report by George Willis of the *New York Post*. 'I did not want them to stop the fight. My strategy was to take it into the seventh and eighth rounds. My strategy was working perfect. I knew his condition was not good. It was not easy, but I felt like I was winning.'

Lewis said: 'He has never been in a dogfight. When the going gets tough, the tough get going.

He stuck in there with me and he made it a good fight.'

It seemed Lewis couldn't win with some members of the American press whatever he did. Vilified in the past for not showing enough aggression, he had done just that against Klitschko and still got criticised.

In a somewhat contrived critique, Dave Anderson of the *New York Times* opined: 'It's in the record book forever. Lewis was knocked out by Rahman and McCall. Now put an asterisk next to his KO6 over Vitali Klitschko. Those three names will haunt Lewis's eventual place in history, just as Buster Douglas haunts Mike Tyson's place in history.

'Whenever boxing buffs measure Lewis against other heavyweight champions, those three names will sabotage his stature. When the best heavyweights of the past lost, it usually was to worthy opponents.'

After 14 years as a professional, Lewis had fought his last fight. He was 37 years old. A rematch was mooted but never came to fruition. According to Klitschko, that was down to one person – Lewis's mother Violet.

'Lennox promised me but his mum decided he wasn't going to fight,' Klitschko told the Press Association in an interview that appeared in *The Guardian* seven years later. 'He invited me to London, without managers. He said he wanted to talk just together. I came to the room and his mum is there. We talked for two hours and his mum was looking at me and scanning me.

'After that, I went away and he called me a couple of hours later and said: "Sorry, but no." I felt it wasn't his decision, his mum decided. I tried to change his decision, but it's difficult.'

In the end, it wasn't difficult for Lewis to walk away. He had beaten every opponent he had faced, achieved all his goals and gone down as the best heavyweight of his era. No one could have asked for more.

Retirement

IN the immediate aftermath of his controversial victory over Vitali Klitschko, a possible mega-money bout with Roy Jones Jr, the former middleweight who had moved up to win a heavyweight title, was also being mentioned.

However, several days later, Lewis then announced that he wanted to meet Klitschko next in a rematch, with 6 December 2003 put forward as a possible date. While he admitted there would be more money on the table for a meeting with Jones, it was the chance to put the record straight against Klitschko that he really wanted.

Despite this, Lewis said he didn't feel as if he would be able to resume training with a view to fighting again at the end of the year. This added further credence to the general consensus that he was intending to retire. For his part, Klitschko said Lewis was looking for a way out of facing him for a second time. It was even announced that the Ukrainian was considering boxing on that date anyway, regardless of whether or nor Lewis was his opponent.

Klitschko, who was becoming increasingly popular with American fight fans, returned to the ring on 6 December to stop the Canadian Kirk Johnson. The WBC then insisted that Lewis made a definite decision on his future by the end of January 2004, or they would strip him of their version of the world title because of inactivity. This deadline was later extended to a new date of 15 March. However, all this proved to be purely academic when at a press conference at the Grosvenor Hotel in London on 6 February 2004, Lennox Lewis, accompanied by members of his team, his mother and fiancée Violet Chang, announced he was retiring from professional boxing. He said: 'It was a long, hard decision to make but at the same time an easy one, because I was looking at doing it a couple of fights back. Should I go back and have one more? But that's the drug of the sport, there's always one more to fight and I didn't want to get caught up in that. I have bowed out as gracefully as I could. In fact, I got sick of people asking me why I was still fighting. There was also a question of hunger and desire and that was the telling blow. If you are not as hungry as I felt against Hasim Rahman the second time, or for Evander Holyfield or Mike Tyson, then it's time to go.'

There was the inevitable question of a possible comeback in the future, but Lewis was adamant he would never come back. 'I have always asked myself why heavyweights retire and come back but I plan to stay out of the ring. I have a new life, a new future. There's more to me than simply being an ex-fighter. It's time for me to say goodbye, so long, see ya, au revoir. I'm happy with my decision. A lot of my backroom team have asked me, including Violet, whether I am sure about quitting and I am because I have pondered for a while.

'I think it is a mistake for any boxer to come back. I liken it to basketball, which I used to play a lot. I packed it up for a while and when I went back I found I couldn't dribble the ball. Those skills had gone and I could not get them back. It always surprises me when guys take so much time out of the ring and then come back. They are only creating needless problems for themselves. I don't need or want those problems.'

When pressed on the subject, Lewis considered his win over Hasim Rahman in their rematch as the best fight of his professional career, explaining, 'The very best has got to be Rahman. Tyson was perhaps the ultimate fight as it had been bugging me for years. Waiting for that fight to happen was what kept me around to a large extent. I was listening to people telling me that Tyson was the best and there was no way that could be true until he fought me. I call the Tyson bout my martial arts fight because I was so focused and close to him in the danger zone, but I was comfortable and whipped him in eight. But with Rahman it was the fact he had disrespected me continually. That really ignited the spark in me and brought the hunger back out.

'Rahman took advantage of his five minutes of fame and pretended he was the heavyweight champion of the world when all I did was loan him the belt. To come back and KO him in four when he knocked me out in five was sweet. It made for a very good Christmas. I enjoyed that one so much. I was serious about the fight. The hunger was there for that one. When I'm in the mood, no one in the world can touch me.'

In summing up his long and successful career, Lewis had no hesitation in stating: 'I was definitely one of the greatest. I dealt with everything with dignity. I did it my way and the end came at the right time.'

Legacy

EXACTLY where Lennox Lewis would be in a list of all-time greatest world heavyweight champions is debatable. Some would argue he was only as successful as he was because of his sheer size and strength.

Whilst he was undoubtedly talented, at times he was prone to losing concentration during bouts and was in the main happy to simply box along at his opponents' pace instead of showing a 'killer instinct'.

However, there were certainly many others who would state that he was a tremendously gifted natural athlete who used his size, strength and superb boxing skills to keep himself out of trouble, while building up the points with his excellent jab.

Anyone questioning his chin should see the heavy shots he absorbed in his bouts with the likes of Gary Mason, Ray Mercer, Evander Holyfield and Andrew Golota, though in reality all such arguments are purely academic. At the end of the day, it all comes down to personal choice and with that, the 'All-Time Greatest' lists of so-called boxing experts are seldom the same. All a boxer can really do is to strive to become the best of his own particular era, and a statistical look at the record of Lennox Lewis certainly proves that he did just that.

In a professional career spanning 14 years, he racked up 41 wins from his 44 contests, with just two defeats and one controversial draw. By his own admission, his two losses were mainly down to a lack of professionalism in terms of underestimating his opponents and maybe not preparing himself as hard as he might have done.

The way in which a fully fit and focused Lewis avenged the defeats in subsequent rematches would tend to bear that out.

Throughout his career, he was always willing to meet, and subsequently beat, all of the top men. Having taken part in 22 title contests, 18 of which were for the world title in one form or another, and taking everything into account, it must be said that not only was Lennox Lewis the best heavyweight of his era, he was also a man who had both the skill and dignity that goes with a truly 'great' heavyweight champion of the world.

Lennox Lewis – Career Record

1989

27 June	Al Malcolm	London, England Won KO 2
21 July	Bruce Johnson	Atlantic City, USA Won TKO 2
25 September	Andy Gerrard	London, England Won TKO 4
10 October	Steve Garber	Hull, England Won TKO 1
5 November	Melvin Epps	London, England Won Disq 2
18 December	Greg Gorrell	Ontario, Canada Won TKO 5

1990

31 January	Noel Quarless	London, England Won KO 2
22 March	Calvin Jones	Gateshead, England Won KO 1
14 April	Mike Simuwelu	London, England Won KO 1
9 May	Jorge Dascola	London, England Won KO 1
20 May	Dan Murphy	Sheffield, England Won TKO 6
27 June	Ossie Ocasio	London, England Won Pts 8
11 July	Mike Acey	Ontario, Canada Won TKO 2
31 October	Jean-Maurice Chanet	London, England Won TKO 6 **EUROPEAN HEAVYWEIGHT TITLE**

1991

6 March	Gary Mason	London, England Won TKO 7

EUROPEAN AND BRITISH HEAVYWEIGHT TITLES

12 July	Mike Weaver	Lake Tahoe, USA Won KO 6
30 September	Glenn McCrory	London, England Won KO 2
23 November	Tyrell Biggs	Atlanta, USA Won TKO 3

1992

1 February	Levi Billups	Las Vegas, USA Won Pts 10
30 April	Derek Williams	London, England Won TKO 3

BRITISH AND EUROPEAN TITLES

11 August	Mike Dixon	Atlantic City, USA Won TKO 4
31 October	Razor Ruddock	London, England Won TKO 2

COMMONWEALTH HEAVYWEIGHT TITLE AND WBC FINAL ELIMINATOR

On 14 December 1992, Lennox Lewis was awarded the WBC world heavyweight title when Riddick Bowe refused to meet him and relinquished that version of the world crown.

1993

8 May	Tony Tucker	Las Vegas, USA
		Won Pts 12
		WBC WORLD TITLE DEFENCE
1 October	Frank Bruno	Cardiff, Wales
		Won TKO 7
		WBC WORLD TITLE DEFENCE

1994

6 May	Phil Jackson	Atlantic City, USA
		Won KO 8
		WBC WORLD TITLE DEFENCE
24 September	Oliver McCall	London, England
		Lost Rsc 2
		WBC WORLD TITLE DEFENCE

1995

13 May	Lionel Butler	Sacramento, USA
		Won TKO 5
		WBC FINAL ELIMINATOR
2 July	Justin Fortune	Dublin, Ireland
		Won TKO 4
7 October	Tommy Morrison	Atlantic City, USA
		Won TKO 6

1996

10 May	Ray Mercer	New York, USA Won Pts 10

1997

7 February	Oliver McCall 2	Las Vegas, USA Won TKO 5 **VACANT WBC WORLD TITLE**
12 July	Henry Akinwande	Lake Tahoe, USA Won Disq 5 **WBC WORLD TITLE DEFENCE**
4 October	Andrew Golota	Atlantic City, USA Won TKO 1 **WBC WORLD TITLE DEFENCE**

1998

28 March	Shannon Briggs	Atlantic City, USA Won TKO 5 **WBC WORLD TITLE DEFENCE**
26 September	Zeljko Mavrovic	Uncasville, USA Won Pts 12 **WBC WORLD TITLE DEFENCE**

1999

13 March	Evander Holyfield	New York, USA
		Drew 12

WBA, IBF AND WBC WORLD TITLE UNIFICATION BOUT

13 November	Evander Holyfield	Las Vegas, USA
		Won Pts 12

WBA, IBF AND WBC WORLD TITLE UNIFICATION BOUT

2000

29 April	Michael Grant	New York, USA
		Won KO 2

WBC AND IBF WORLD TITLE DEFENCES

15 July	Frans Botha	London, England
		Won TKO 2

WBC AND IBF WORLD TITLE DEFENCES

11 November	David Tua	Las Vegas, USA
		Won Pts 12

WBC AND IBF WORLD TITLE DEFENCES

2001

2w April	Hasim Rahman	J.burg, S.Africa
		Lost KO 5

WBC AND IBF WORLD TITLE DEFENCES

17 November	Hasim Rahman	Las Vegas, USA
		Won KO 4

WBC AND IBF WORLD TITLES

2002

8 June	Mike Tyson	Las Vegas, USA
		Won KO 8

WBC AND IBF WORLD TITLE DEFENCES

2003

21 June	Vitali Klitschko	Los Angeles, USA
		Won TKO 6

WBC AND IBF WORLD TITLE DEFENCES

On 6 February 2004, Lennox Lewis relinquished his world titles and retired from boxing with an official record of 41 wins from 44 contests, two defeats and one draw, with 32 victories inside the distance.

Sources Of Information

With the vast majority of the information contained in this work having been accurately obtained from that which was freely available at the time of each particular contest, it must be pointed out that certain established boxing trade magazines including *Boxing News*, *Boxing Monthly*, and also the short-lived *Boxing Weekly*, are extremely useful sources of information relating to the career of Lennox Lewis and should rightly be acknowledged as being so.